The Streets of Laredo Politics

Justin Allen Hundsnurscher

The Streets of Laredo Politics

ISBN: 978-1-329-78571-7

Third Edition

justinforlaredo@gmail.com

Copyright © 2015, 2016, 2017, 2018, 2019 Justin Allen Hundsnurscher

This writing is dedicated to my grandfather, the late Jorge Casiano, Sr. and the late great Laredo Mayor Aldo Tatangelo

ACKNOWLEDGEMENTS

This writing is a composition of current and past events relating to those in public and elected office. Information has been gathered from multiple media information, personal experiences, Internet media postings, and personal databases. While some of the views and opinions are expressed by the writer, not all writings are the ultimate opinion of the writer and are based on the events of which have occurred.

DISCLAIMER

The opinions and events mentioned herein are not intended to influence or manipulate anyone by any manner. Neither the writer nor any other person mentioned in the writing may be held liable for any damages that can result. The reader is to make his or her own opinion and mindset upon reading this writing. Readers are encouraged to make their own determination and seek further investigation into any matter, event, or opinion set forth in this writing.

CONTENTS

PROLOGUE

Chapter 1:   **Page 8**
THE START OF THE PATRÓN PARTY AND JC "PEPE" MARIN RULE
    LBJ and The Old Party

Chapter 2:   **Page 14**
REMINISCENCES OF THE PAST
    Washington's Birthday celebration

Chapter 3:   **Page 17**
ALDO TATANGELO

Chapter 4:   **Page 20**
POLITICS AFTER TATANGELO ERA

Chapter 5:   **Page 26**
THE SECOND MINI REVOLUTION

Chapter 6:   **Page 28**
FAMILY TIES

Chapter 7:   **Page 31**
"CORRUPTION" IN POLITICS
    A "Democrat" Webb County?
    Employment in City & County
    Pay increases for elected officials
    Misuse of power?
    Naming of parks and public places
    Contributions to stay elected
    Lemurs closure

Chapter 8:   **Page 39**
CORRUPTION AND UNETHICAL CASES
    Triple Ax Smiley case
    City Secretary sexual harassment
    Drugs and politics
    Dirty water
    Solicitation of a minor
    Commissioner's bribes
    Raffle money
    Police chief bribe
    Sexual harassment
    Justice of the Peace bribery

Taking signs
Rio Bravo mayor
County Attorney's office
County Court at Law II
The FBI Raid

Chapter 9:   **Page 55**
CAÑONEROS

Chapter 10:   **Page 59**
POLITICAL GROUPS AND CONTROL

Chapter 11:   **Page 61**
ARE THE VOTERS GUILTY OF CORRUPTION?

Chapter 12:   **Page 63**
ISSUES IN LAREDO AND WHY VOTING MATTERS
          The issues matter
          Turned off voters?
          Heated races and political controversy
          Charter initiative

Chapter 13:   **Page 73**
VOTES DO MATTER

Chapter 14:   **Page 75**
TRUMP'S LAREDO VISIT

Chapter 15:   **Page 77**
INTEREST IN LOCAL POLITICS

Chapter 16:   **Page 79**
MY CAMPAIGN IN 2014

Chapter 17:   **Page 85**
MY LETTER TO THE EDITORS

Chapter 18:   **Page 88**
MY CAMPAIGN IN 2016

Chapter 19:   **Page 93**
MY CAMPAIGN IN 2018

EPILOGUE

ABOUT THE AUTHOR

BIBLIOGRAPHY

PROLOGUE

Everyone drives the streets of Laredo, the old rugged roadways to the newly paved darkened streets, and some man-made dirt roads. All roads lead to downtown, the place where the "*politicos*" meet and decide what to bring in fruition.

Corruption in Webb County and Laredo did not begin spontaneously; with an over 160-year history of rulers and corruption cases, there seems to be no end in sight. The hunger for money, greed, and power mostly leads to the corruption and unethical behavior we have seen throughout our decades.

Because of the culture of an elected official, once someone gets into the position they were running for, many people come forth to them and need something from this official. This is when some of the corruption can evolve.

Sometimes the electorate is guilty of the corruption occurring in our community because at times they are offered jobs or can benefit in some form if their candidate becomes elected. Would you bite the hand that feeds?

Some of the time, it is not truly about corruption but rather just the culture of local politics and the way it has been for centuries. This writing is not solely focusing on corruption but on the political plays in Laredo and Webb County politics. One needs to know how to play the game if he wants in per say.

In truth, there are many forms of political corruption in our local community such bribery, extortion, embezzlement, nepotism, and the patronage or *patrón* system that we see so prevalent. A *patrón* system of government consists of granting political favors, contracts, or appointments to various positions by an elected official or candidate for office in exchange for political support.

Laredo is a big city of a quarter of a million people with a small-town political mentality. Our city is the main hub of the United States largest inland customs district and is the 10th largest city in the State of Texas. Included in our city is a large student population at Texas A&M International University with over 95% of residents being Hispanic and Latino, being one of the least ethnically diverse cities in the United States.

An outlet mall opened in downtown Laredo, and expansions all around our city can be seen everywhere with many new neighborhoods and businesses popping up all over town.

Unfortunately, Laredo also has one of the largest poverty rates in Texas as almost 30% of residents living below the poverty level. Sixty eight percent of the population has a high school diploma, and the median household income in 2016 was at $35,195. There are areas of the county where residents do not have access to running water and sewer connections, much less paved streets in the *colonias*.

Independent studies have also shown that in the span of just two years between 2018 and 2019, Laredo was ranked the least affordable city in Texas for homeowners and renters. Additionally, other studies showed the Gateway City ranked second in the nation with food stamp usage. According to WalletHub, Laredo is also a city in the state with the highest concentration of poverty rate, the worst city to raise a family, the worst city to live an active lifestyle, and worst city to be single.

This writing was not an easy one to write because being how small our community is, some of the names, people, and interactions mentioned are known personally. Many of the names have even supported my campaigns at one point or another and I have voted for. The experiences of running three campaigns and understanding the history of our political system have made this writing needed. This is not a writing to be proud of because some of the things mentioned but must be written so we may learn from the past, the present, and better our future.

The difficulty of writing some of the occurrences mentioned hit close at times and will to many, whether personally or from someone they know. With this in mind, every detail had to be placed as it is and let history judge in the end. Many of the people in this writing does not mean I am against or for them; it is what it is. Ensured was to not leave anything out based on any personal opinions on any given issue or view. The people have to know the history.

Chapter 1:

THE START OF THE PATRÓN PARTY AND JC "PEPE" MARTIN RULE

El patrón or *El Partido Viejo,* known as the "Old Party" or the Independent Club was no secret in the border city of Laredo, Texas. Former Laredo Mayor Joseph Claude "J.C." Martin ruled the city through his term from 1954 through 1978. Martin was known for his political grandstanding by performing political favors to the public and would in return receive absolute political loyalty. Before elected mayor, Martin served as District Clerk in the 49th Judicial District.

He was no stranger to politics as his father, the senior, was a businessman rancher and a Webb County Sheriff. His father also served as president of the Laredo Independent School District. His uncle, Albert Martin also had served as Laredo's Mayor.

Becoming mayor, Martin continued the family realm by becoming the 11th descendant of Don Tomas Sanchez, Laredo's founder and mayor. In the 1954 election, Martin ran unopposed and had only one write-in vote cast against him for O.W. Killam.

Martin won six consecutive terms for Mayor where an era of no term limits existed. He decided against running for a seventh term in 1978 when business owner Aldo Tatangelo ran and eventually became elected.

The San Agustin Plaza in downtown Laredo part of where the attack reportedly took place.

History would be kind to the Old Party as the evolution of this club came about because of the 1894 *Botas* and *Guaraches* conflict, otherwise known as the boots and sandals. A *patrón* of grand standards of politics and the wealth of no one else on the border, Raymond Martin ruled the *Botas*. The *Guaraches* included then Webb County Judge Jose Maria Rodriguez; a person of wealth too, but still was able to draw support from lower class individuals. Through its years in power, the *Botas* obtained political power by running most of the county precincts. With the history of illegal votes, in a very close city election of 1886, the two "parties" would come to a clash. The *Botas* would once again win this year but riots erupted between both the *Botas* and *Guaraches*. The *Botas* celebrated their victory on April 7, 1886, in the streets of Laredo with a parade. With this win, the *Botas* hoped to end and kill the *Guaraches* reign forever. However, the *Guaraches* attacked the parade in downtown Laredo held by the *Botas* and became one of the largest gun battles in the

American West. Soldiers stationed at Fort McIntosh restored order by declaring martial law. Over 250 men were reported to be involved in the fight with numerous deaths and injuries resulting in the riot.

The battle would not leave permanent scars, however, as both the *Botas* and *Guaraches* joined forces in 1887 against the Texas Prohibition Party and a year later would form the Laredo Immigration and Improvement Society.

In 1895, people from both ex-revivals united to form the Independent Club, known as the "*Partido Viejo*" as we know it today. This regime would officially dominate the politics of Laredo until the end of the JC "Pepe" Martin era in 1978.

The headquarters of the "*Partido Viejo*" was located on Jarvis Plaza in downtown Laredo. The Independent Club as it was named controlled all factions of the local electorate from the city, county, and even the local schools. Members included lawyers, businessmen, and several citizens who depended financially on the *patrón* system. Funds would be raised to run different campaigns and elect their people into offices in city, county, state, and even federal level.

Notable individuals elected and appointed to offices from this system were; Antonio M. Bruni, a Webb County Treasurer and County Commissioner; and Albert Martin son of Raymond Martin was chosen as Mayor of Laredo in 1926. Others included Harold R. Yeary and Dr. Leonides Gonzalez Cigarroa, both LISD trustees.

Under the *patrón* system, those loyal to the party would be granted jobs in local government, including positions with the police, fire, and the schools for Laredo Independent School District. In particular, those with large families would get preferential treatment for employment, as they would deliver the votes for the *patrón* party. These votes were in a way, controlled, and those associated would say they could have a source of pride or importance for knowing they can deliver Martin his votes.

You see, with the high amount of poverty in those days, the *patrón* party could control their people by manipulation. The largest employers at the time were public entities with the city, county, and the lone school district – Laredo ISD. All public entities had over 5,000 people employed, meaning those were fully affected by the old *patrón* party, thus had to comply with them to keep their jobs.

Many were unskilled workers, which were easy to be manipulated according to the party. However, professionals, such as teachers were also affected. Those hired for teaching and in administrative positions for the schools were political rewards for those who displayed patronage to the Old Party. J.W. Nixon was the superintendent during the Old Party days, and many of the decisions occurred as a result of politics.

According to Fernando Piñon's *Patron Democracy*, a traffic captain for the Laredo Police Department at the time achieved his position for being loyal to the Old Party. Stating, "The party has been good to me, and I intend to continue working for the party. I am not an educated man. I did not go to college, but still, I am second in command of the police department. You must learn how to play the game. You take care of the party, and the party will take care of you."

Many other positions were given to individuals with no skills or educational background for the position they were hired to do. Many said they did not have a degree but earning much more than one who did and had to go along with the Old Party to get ahead.

There was no surprise that Martin's fall would eventually succumb as in 1977 a man by the name of Lawrence Berry spearheaded an organization named the Taxpayers for Public Service (TOPS). He investigated records and audits noticing many discrepancies. An audit of the street department showed the city dispensed 15,000 gallons a month of gas, enough for everyone in residing in Laredo. Furthermore, Martin placed a bank vice-president on the payroll as a street inspector, including other phantom employees being paid on taxpayer dollars. Berry also noticed 906 car batteries were purchased in a 16-month period for 87 active vehicles at the time. Ultimately, he discovered over half of a million dollars of fraud in the street department.

Berry owned a printing shop and lived in Laredo for only ten years before speaking against JC Martin's administration.

On June 20, 1978, CBS broadcast a nationally televised interview where reporter Bill Moyers interviewed Berry and Martin. The interview titled "You Can Beat City Hall" brought forth the corruption from the *patrón* of the city in Laredo. Moyers called the political system of Laredo, "ruled by a family of patrons, rich, powerful, and unbeatable."

Martin owned 70,000 acres of ranch land worth an estimated ten million dollars at the time, mainly from big gas and oil. Martin's political machine grew because of his ability to control and manipulate low-income impoverished people who could not speak English.

Martin described the *patrón* system to Moyers as "one man, two men, or a group of men having control" of jobs, businesspeople, and stores. The *patrón* party controlled many thousand votes and would influence races in all aspects of elections within the city, county, state and even federal. Martin had stated barbecue parties before elections were an effective method to have a pre-election rally and get everyone to go and vote, thus controlling their votes.

According to the CBS interview, during his tenure at the time, Laredo had 80,000 residents, 4 out of 5 spoke Spanish better than English, almost half of the residents lived below the poverty line, the per capita income less than $2,300 at the time, one out of every three residents received food stamps, and the local unemployment rate at the time was at 15 percent. Millions of federal dollars were brought in through good connections, but minimal was to show for in the streets of Laredo where many streets were unpaved. This was unchallenged and the norm for Laredo.

Martin's power of the *Patrón* Party was seen diminishing in the later years of his term especially when legislation on the War on Poverty that was signed by President Lyndon B. Johnson in January of 1964. The legislation required a governing body to be comprised that included public officials, civic organizations, and representatives from the poor. Of course, Martin would attempt to control the War on Poverty program from its inception being appointed chairman and sought to hire individuals associated with the Independent Club, such as Billy Hall, Jr. being the public information officer, and other individuals who worked well with Martin's system such as Hector Farias and Blas Martinez. However, the War on Poverty required appointments of three categories, and the third, representatives of the poor are what gave Martin trouble. Before, Martin's *Patrón* Party strived on controlling the poor, however with the War on Poverty the poor were gaining power and a say at the table. The initiative gave rise to several activists such as Manuel "Chaca" Ramirez, Guillermo C. Perez, and Jose A. Valdez, who would be elected councilman in the 90's and later an LISD trustee. Martin attempted to manipulate the War on Poverty board, which was carried out through the Economic Opportunities Development Corporation (EODC), but his influence could only be contained at least through the mid 1970's. Martin continued to be re-elected as Mayor in 1966, 1970, and 1974. He received some opposition that he did not previously see in the 1970 race where his opponent, Tomas Flores received 1,472 votes against Martin's 8,260 and in 1974, 5,170 votes were received compared to his opponent, Harvill Eaton's 783 votes.

Martin was able to hold on as Mayor in 1970 because of his political moves such as when Jose A. Valdez resigned as chairman of the board for the War on Poverty and took a job as executive director for the agency. The move was a political gift for Martin, however Valdez did not intend it to be this way.

Valdez's resignation gave Martin more control over the board on the War on Poverty. Although Martin was re-elected in 1974, there were signs of political rebellion as in 1972 Angel Laurel won the district attorney seat running against Fred Bruni, Martin's first cousin and member of the Old Party. Laurel's brother Oscar had previously been district attorney and an ally of the Old Party.

After the early 1972 elections, Martin's power had shrunk to only the city as county offices that previously saw Old Party loyalist was no longer seen. Martin could no longer defend his corruption within the city.

After Martin's re-election in 1974, a man by the name of Aldo Tatangelo had done so much for the community that there were talks of him running for political office. Tatangelo often attended council meetings and found many discrepancies in city run business such as numerous unpaved roads where Laredo had a budget of $10.5 million compared to Mc Allen's $5.7 million. Martin would not be able to justify the over half million dollars allocated for the street department; he could not defend the high number of people on the payroll who were phantom employees. He could no longer do what he could years before because he was being exposed.

Similarity the Old Party was falling apart as loyalist were now running against each other or running without Martin's blessing. As the mayoral election of 1978 neared, Martin saw Old Party loyalist defeated in the sheriff's office when Mario Santos won in 1976 and Tatangelo constantly kept going before council asking questions with receiving deceptive answers. He kept persisting and with time, more people grew in attendance at the council meetings that would normally be empty. Tatangelo would see he was gaining followers and people from the *barrios* such as those in *La Ladrillera*. The tenacity and leadership that Tatangelo showed is what eventually led him running for mayor and winning. Martin did not run for re-election in 1978 and opened the door to six candidates - Tatangelo being one. Tatangelo's strongest opponent was Oscar M. Laurel who was supported by the Old Party. Tatangelo received 9,748 votes with Laurel receiving 4,833.

After the election of Tatangelo most of the remnants of the Martin political era were diminishing with E. James Kazen being defeated for the position of 49th District Court Judge. Honore Ligarde fell ill and quit during his race for County Court-at-law Judge, however in the 1978 elections, some managed to be elected such as C.Y. Benavides II who won as County Judge, a nephew of Martin, and Dr. Hector Farias won the race for county treasurer, and for county clerk, Enrique Flores, a nephew of former Sheriff Porfirio L. Flores won his race.

Ultimately, because of the efforts of Lawrence Berry and other brave individuals, Joseph Claude Martin, Jr. was indicted by a federal grand jury in 1978 on a single count of mail fraud. Martin pleaded guilty, and a $1,000 fine was paid, including $201,118 in restitution to the city of Laredo for the usage of city employees on Martin's private properties. He further served thirty weekends in the Webb County Jail, the very same jail that Martin's father helped build as sheriff. Martin told the judge as he stood before him, "I pray for your understanding and your consideration."

Many felt the sentence was light considering all the corruption Martin caused Laredo for many decades.

Berry called politicians servants stating, "I don't work for them, they work me." And urged the people to watch the government and let them serve you.

"You have to have some loyal opposition… hopefully the candidate we get in there, some of them will be for the better, some of them will be as crooked as the ones we have now, that's just the name of the game, that's democracy, hopefully we don't have to be stuck with the crooked for another 100 years, in the next election we can kick them out."

He further stated regarding the future, "It isn't going to be any kind of wonderland... but at least we'll have some for solving it. We were stuck for nearly a century in one system and no way out."

He brought down the system, then.

Martin did not fully take responsibility for the corruption on phantom employees and malfunctioning sewage plant. He stated, "Well, I had suspicion to this degree that the expenses kept going up, kept going up" and when question this he was told the "city services were increasing and knew they were because of the growing population and keep up, but that's about as far as I can take responsibility for that."

In 1979, resulting from the long-tenured control on the city, Tatangelo and the city council went from a strong mayoral system of government to a city council-manager government.

Martin admittedly stated the voters did not have a democracy during the Old Party reign and would now have one in the 1978 mayoral election.

Mayor Martin lived a lengthy life after his takedown where he called a large white house with Corinthian columns home. The home still stands on Clark Boulevard and Meadow Street. Martin died on November 11, 1998 at a San Antonio hospital after a back injury from a fall at his home. He is buried in the Calvary Catholic Cemetery in Laredo, Texas.

Upon his death, many Laredoans praised his contributions to the city. In a 1998 *Laredo Morning Times* article, several local leaders praised Martin, including a nephew, the now deceased Billy Hall Jr., a former Texas State Representative and Webb County Treasurer. Max Mandel, a former banker, and civic leader stated Martin was good to local banks because of his implementations of policies as a board member of the bank he ran. Vidal M. Trevino, a former State Representative and Laredo ISD Superintendent, stated Martin "was one of a kind, the most outstanding individual of Laredo in this century."

Trevino was another member of the Independent Club and helped dominate the political scene through the help of former Sheriff J.C. Martin, Sr., Mayor JC Martin, Jr., District Attorney Phillip Kazen, and U.S. Congressman Abraham Kazen.

Many dispute if his legacy of corruption has died with him or has continued with a new brand of *el patrón* politics. While Martin may have done the most damage to this South Texas community, there is doubt he was not the one who started the regime or ended it.

LBJ and the Old Party

The Old Party, or the *Partido Viejo* was not exclusive to Laredo and Webb County as the surrounding county of Duval and Jim Wells County had "The Duke of Duval" or "*El Patrón*" otherwise known as George Parr. Parr was a member of the Democratic political machine that controlled Duval and Jim Wells County, and some say essentially gave Lyndon B. Johnson the presidency. Parr served as Duval County Judge and Sheriff, but most importantly, he controlled politics in the form of bribes, graft, and illegal donations.

In 1932 Parr was convicted of income tax evasion, in which he was in prison for nine months, but then pardoned in 1946, by President Harry Truman.

Reports were that Parr was pardoned with the help of several Texas politicians, including Lyndon B. Johnson, a U.S. Representative at the time.

When Johnson ran for the U.S. Senate in 1948, the election was so close that Johnson was able to win by only 87 votes. Jim Wells County was the key factor as Johnson's opponent had a 112-vote lead, but then the county amended their returns adding 202 more votes and 200 of those being for Johnson, thus giving Johnson an 87-vote lead. Some say Parr used his influence to affect the vote tally in Johnson's favor as he had helped Parr get the 1946 pardon.

The Laredo connection is not just the *Partido Viejo*'s South Texas politics, but what makes this stranger is that a likely motivation to oppose Johnson's opponent, Coke R. Stevenson in the Senate race is how Stevenson as Governor in 1944 failed to appoint E. James Kazen as district attorney. Parr and Judge Manuel Raymond had asked Stevenson to appoint Kazen (a relative of Raymond). Observers say this turned Parr to control the vote for Johnson and the rest is history. Parr died by suicide in 1975 a year after being convicted of income tax evasion and sentenced a ten-year prison term in which he could not got away with.

The machine that helped Johnson was still active when Johnson became president after the tragic Kennedy assassination in 1963. Being a native Texan and teacher in Cotulla, Johnson knew about the political machines running south Texas and when Johnson became president, Martin realized this. Martin knew Johnson on a first name basis and satisfied he had a friend in Washington that many years ago helped a fellow *patrón*, Parr be pardoned and had an appeal reversed by the Supreme Court in 1960 after a conviction of income tax evasion and mail fraud.

However, as we know, Johnson initiated the War on Poverty that eventually caused the demise of Martin's political rule.

Chapter 2:

REMINISCENCES OF THE PAST

Although the leaders of the past *Partido Viejo* have been gone for many years now, most of their namesakes still exist and are prominent in the city. A drive through the streets of Laredo, one will be able to see the Bruni Plaza and Bruni Elementary School, named after Antonio M. Bruni. A school, such as Martin High School in the Laredo Independent School District is named after JC Martin's grandparents, Raymond and Tirza Martin. JC Martin Elementary and Honore Ligarde Elementary School are other LISD campuses named after the former mayor and his brother-in-law, respectively.

Families of those in the Old Party have been prominent in contemporary politics.

JC Martin, Jr. had a daughter married to Dr. Michael V. Galo, who is a brother to former Councilman and County Commissioner John C. Galo. Former County Judge and Councilman Louis H. Bruni is an uncle of Martin, who publicly admitted in the 1990's he wanted to dismantle the two linked institutions with his family. Bruni fought against the political

J.C. Martin Elementary located in central Laredo.

machine of Martin and the *patrón* of the past, Bruni's father, Frederick Bruni. JC Martin, Jr.'s uncle Billy Hall, Jr. served as a State Representative and County Treasurer. Hall's great-grandfather was Antonio M. Bruni, a former Webb County Treasurer as well.

Today, the Webb County Administrative Building is named after Billy Hall, Jr., including a bronze bust of him in the building. The Laredo Community College named its student center after him at its south campus.

Cigarroa High School was named after Dr. Leonides Gonzalez Cigarroa, a former LISD trustee who was supported by the Old Party. Also, Laredo College named their library in the downtown campus after Harold R. Yeary, another former LISD Trustee supported by the Old Party.

We will know the engraving of past names and legacies from our past undeniable history. Whether we agree with the past "*patrón system*" or not, history is recorded and there for individuals to learn and implement their values.

Washington's Birthday Celebration

The most significant celebration in Laredo every year is not Christmas, Halloween, or even New Year's Eve, it is well, the George Washington Birthday Celebration.

While the majority of U.S. cities do not bother to celebrate the first President of the United States, George Washington, Laredo observes his birthday every year in grand celebrations. Local school districts even provide a holiday to their students and staff to celebrate.

The history of the Washington Birthday Celebration or WBCA as it is also known was first celebrated by a fraternal organization from San Antonio called the Improved Order of Red Men, in which they established a local chapter, Yaqui Tribe #59 in 1898. Historians say the Anglo fraternity sensed they needed to be reminded of how they were in the United States and not Mexico. When they arrived in Laredo, many Mexican American families hold onto land and had Mexican customs with a feeling of being in Mexico. The fraternity introduced the celebration as a form of reminder they were still in the United States. Until the inception of Washington's Birthday Celebration, Laredoans celebrated its major holidays of *Cinco de Mayo* and *Diez y Seis de Septiembre*.

Also, before this, former mayor of Laredo Samuel Jarvis organized a smaller version of the celebration in his home. The celebration officially received its state charter in 1923 and featured their first Colonial Pageant in 1939.

In the beginning, members of the Yaqui Tribe #59 would stage a mock battle on city hall against the mayor, city council, police force, and citizens where men would dress as Native Americans in costumes with painted faces where Indians would attack innocent Anglo and Mexican settlers. The mayor would then turn over the key of the city surrendering to the state leader of the Improved Order of Red Men when the Indians would defeat the settlers. After that, a parade, pageant and burlesque show would be held with an ending reenacting the Boston Tea Party.

Now, the celebration is a multi-week event known as delightful and extravagant full of entertainment, food, and activities. Kids enjoy the crazy rides of the carnival, adults the music and food of the Jalapeno Festival, and both young and old enjoy the visuals of the parades. Most have always been this way, but before the throw down of the *Partido Viejo*, this celebration was more of a different kind than just festive and entertaining.

Oilmen, bankers, ranchers, congressional representatives, and other politicians would gather every year to celebrate Washington's Birthday Celebration and reap the rewards from their fellow kind. In 1939, The Martha Washington Society was an addition to the Washington's Birthday Celebration hosting the Colonial Pageant and Ball. The celebration included the extravagant balls with expensive gowns and costumes, and as journalist Bill Moyers pointed, they celebrated with the "power that belonged to a close circle of the privileged." This was a social event where not any ordinary person could participate in, different from the current celebration, as we know it today.

By the 1990's those participating in pageants spent an average of $20,000 on gowns which many said were only catered to the high social class in Laredo where most of its citizens made less a year than the cost of a gown.

Still celebrated is part of the prominent man and woman who play George and Martha Washington, which also consists of Mr. South Texas. Honore Ligarde was Washington's Birthday Association president in 1962 who succeeded Vidal M. Treviño; past recipients of the Mr. South Texas award have included politicians, oilmen, bankers, and ranchers, including; Mayor JC Martin, Jr.; Senator John Cornyn; two relatives of the Killam family Oliver Winfield Killam and Radcliffe Killam in 1956 and 1978, respectively; and President George W. Bush.

In 2016, Minnie Dora Bunn Haynes, a great-granddaughter of former Mayor JC Martin portrayed Martha Washington at The Society of Martha Washington Colonial Pageant & Ball, an event by the WBCA.

Today, the George Washington Birthday celebration events combined attract thousands of residents and visitors and contribute millions of dollars to the local economy. Scholarships are also awarded through Mr. South Texas. We see the 'abrazo' ceremony at the International Bridge where officials from Mexico and the United States exchange hugs in welcoming them symbolizing the amity and understanding between the two neighboring countries.

Carlos Garza, a volunteer for the celebration says Washington "was so revered in the United States and Mexico that we honor him." Washington is not only the first U.S. President, but also a symbol for the people regarding freedom and their love of American history.

Laredo is now in the spotlight of the nation where each February the George Washington's Birthday Celebration is considered the oldest celebration honoring President Washington. There is no doubt this yearly celebration is a positive one for the community, on the other hand, with the history of this event we must also recognize the politics of it.

Chapter 3:

ALDO TATANGELO

Aldo Tatangelo served as Laredo mayor from 1978 through 1990. He preceded Jose C. "Pepe" Martin, Jr. (1954-1978) and was succeeded by Saul N. Ramirez, Jr. (1990-1997).

"One might think that the Mayor of this border city, which is 92 percent Mexican-American, would have a name like Garcia or Lopez or be a descendant of the gunslingers who once shot up its famous streets. In fact, the Mayor of Laredo is an Italian-American from Rhode Island". Those were the words of a 1985 *New York Times* article mentioning the Mayor Aldo Tatangelo's tenure.

Aldo Tatangelo was originally going to run for city council, but after Lawrence Berry spoke out at a city council meeting against JC "Pepe" Martin, unsettling a councilman, a supporter of Martin. The councilman chastised Tataneglo and Berry at a city council meeting, stating all they were really doing by their "so-called public outcry is to conduct a political campaign for self and Aldo Tatangelo." The councilman suggested they do it on their own time and own expense. He further stated, "We do not have time to continue to listen to the same old rhetoric, we do not recognize you are representing the community or public in general." Berry fired back, "Sir, in reference to in running for city council since you brought the issue up, he's running for mayor, he has the guts that he's running, do you?" The public broke out in applause while the councilman, smoking a cigarette asked "do you want to ask me out outside?" and stated, "I respect the council here, and it's the second time you insult me if you insult me outside it would be a different story, friend." Sounding much like Al Pacino in *Scarface*.

Grave site in the Laredo cemetery

Tatangelo was born in *Diez y Seis de Septiembre* in 1913 in Providence, Rhode Island far away from the grand celebrations we see on the border on the 16th of September.

Tatangelo joined the U.S. Navy in 1943 during World War II and served as a fireman 1st class but was honorably discharged and a year later he opened his business in Rhode Island.

He lived in Mexico City for five years after moving there in 1958 to expand his business supervising its plant operations of sunglasses. According to the *Laredo Morning Times*, he always felt like a foreigner in Mexico, saying "I liked the city, but I didn't think it was a place for my children to grow up in." Tatangelo could not speak his mind much in Mexico and in Laredo he could and did. He chose to reside in Laredo, and as he crossed from Mexico to the U.S. in 1963, he found out about the Kennedy assassination upon seeing the U.S. flag at half-mast in Laredo.

The assassination affected Tataneglo in sadness and in business success where the sales of Kennedy medallions became popular at the time and Tatangelo and his wife decided to create necklaces that included the medallions. He saw an opportunity in the retail business in Laredo with the sale of the medallion necklaces and partnered with a professor from Laredo Junior College to form a business named Frontier Novelty Company.

While in Laredo, Tatangelo enjoyed the people and the close-knit community of Laredo. He liked how people were courteous and civil. So much so, that had yearned to help the people of Laredo and recruited several volunteers in 1973 to build a fire station on Del Mar Boulevard.

The business was becoming prosperous by the day as Tatangelo reaped the benefits of a healthy and expanded Mexican economy as a downtown merchant. Before becoming politically active, Tatangelo was active in the professional and business community. His political interest in local politics began when he grew active in the Day Care Centers Program of the Community Action Agency. It was there where he saw the bureaucracy of the War on Poverty initiative and how it was controlled by Martin's regime. He began to ask questions and notice Laredo was at least 50 years behind the times.

Seeing how the streets of Laredo were mostly unpaved in the late 1970's, how the council was a rubber-stamped council, and the math was not adding up to the city's budget expenditures, Tatangelo challenged the city administration, thus becoming involved in local politics. He told the *Laredo Morning Times*, "Laredo was such a closed city. There was a clique, and if you were part of it, you were O.K., but if you weren't, then things were not so good."

Tatangelo said he lost 25 pounds campaigning for mayor and visited 10,100 residences; he eventually won the race for Mayor in April of 1978 where he served three terms as mayor through 1990. Tatangelo said his election was a new beginning with new ideas and new things to do.

Upon taking office, Tatangelo offered a new sense of relief to the citizens of Laredo after the decades-old control of a savvy political corrupt party. The Gateway City as it is known saw accountability by efforts resulting in changes such as a street-paving program so comprehensive that many say brought the city into the 20th century. Most of the streets of Laredo were not on par with other areas of such a population, many being unpaved dirt roads. Laredo also saw many significant infrastructure improvements.

No longer was the mayor entirely in charge as the political boss as the city council adopted a system where it went from a strong mayoral system of government to a city council-manager government; thus, a new city charter was in place with these changes.

Under Tatangelo's watch, the city of Laredo also saw a reorganization of the much-corrupted city street department. He was also credited for developing the parks and recreation department (now known as the parks and leisure); creating a planning and zoning commission comprised of individuals in public; promoted affordable housing for low-income Laredoans; and championed pensions for city employees. Laredo also saw a stronger bond with Nuevo Laredo's officials.

Tatangelo was not much of a Spanish speaker having an Italian accent; but this never hindered his support from Laredoans and was widely popular during his time as mayor. He told the *New York Times* many local residents named their sons for him, Aldo, claiming, "There are a lot of little Aldos running around now."

A former city councilman, Joe Guerra said Tatangelo was so open with the public that anyone could visit him at his office or home regardless of status or without an appointment.

After his three terms as mayor of Laredo, Tatangelo campaigned as a write-in candidate for Webb County Judge in 1990 to challenge the Democratic nominee; Mercurio Martinez, Jr. Tatangelo could not garner enough votes as a write-in candidate, and Martinez won with 75% of the vote. Martinez previously ran unsuccessfully against Tatangelo in 1982 as he served as a city councilman. Mercurio Martinez was known as an "Old Party loyalist" and considered "the best Old Party candidate to reclaim the mayorship" at the time, according to the book titled *Patron Democracy* by Fernando Piñon.

By 1998, Tatangelo started to diminish in his health after open-heart surgery. He told the public he wanted to stay publicly active, but his physicians advised him not to because of his health, further saying he missed not being able to sit down and figure our problems in the city.

Tatangelo died on March 7, 2008, at the Golden age of 94 and buried in Laredo at the Catholic Calvary Cemetery and while his legacy has remained strong, no schools are named after him – yet, unlike the individuals involved with the *Partido Viejo*. However, the city honored him with the "Aldo Tatangelo Parkway" in downtown Laredo. In 2008, city council voted to name city hall after him, but the name change was never made. In the fall of 2019, city council again discussed changing the name of City Hall to Aldo Tatangelo, but some council members disagreed saying that although Tatangelo contributed much to Laredo, city hall should not be named to any elected official as it is for the people.

Before the election of Aldo Tataneglo, Laredo was still living in the 19th century, and his leadership was the cause of Laredo moving forward into the 20th century and beyond the 21st century. People plagued with fear of voting the wrong way or feared for retaliation if something was said they could not under the *Partido Viejo,* and the new mayor changed that under his watch.

Tatangelo's son spoke on his father's rosary saying, "My dad and Laredo had a love affair for thirty-five years. They loved him; he loved them. They broke the mold when they made Aldo. There will never be another one. It's interesting when a man can have that kind of a feeling for a city, and the city return it." He said his father "set Laredo free and changed how people thought..." pointing Laredo in a new direction and wanted it open and prosperous. Further saying many were "fearful of doing the wrong thing or of getting fired if they voted for the wrong person or if they said or did the wrong thing."

Tatangelo Jr. died two years after his father's passing.

Chapter 4:

POLITICS AFTER TATANGELO ERA

In 1990, Laredo elected a new mayor, Saul N. Ramirez, Jr. becoming the youngest elected mayor in Laredo history at the age of 31. Tatangelo could not run for another term as the city charter was changed during his tenure and term limits were implemented. The newly elected Ramirez was elected in a run-off between Maria "Bebe" Zuniga and himself. He previously served as a city councilman for two terms. Ramirez served two-terms and vacated his seat in 1997 as he was appointed to the deputy secretary of the United States Secretary of Housing and Urban Development position under the William J. Clinton administration in Washington, D.C.

City Council in the mid-1990's consisted of several elected officials who later served in other elected offices or ran unsuccessfully for elected offices. Both Jose R. Perez and Cecilia May Moreno would later serve as Laredo Independent School District trustees, and Louis H. Bruni would serve as Webb County Judge. Consuelo "Chelo" Montalvo and Alfonso "Poncho" Casso would run for several campaigns unsuccessfully. John C. Galo, a councilman, elected in 1998 would run for mayor unsuccessfully in 2006 and ran successfully to be elected Webb County Commissioner in 2012.

1998 saw a wind of change in mayoral politics in Laredo as it once again made history electing the first female mayor. Elizabeth "Betty" Garcia Flores would be elected after Ramirez vacated his seat. She defeated Councilman "Poncho" Casso and Attorney Fausto Sosa. Oddly, Betty Flores was a neighbor as a child to former Mayor J.C "Pepe" Martin, Jr. After twenty years leaving office would he then see Flores as Laredo's Mayor.

Flores's father was Eloy Garcia, Sr. a businessman philanthropist and a Laredo Community College Board of Trustee and mother Bonnie Lopez, who donated land to the United Independent School District to build Bonnie L. Garcia Elementary School.

The accomplishments of Flores include; airport improvements; the creation of the Laredo arena; a new police headquarters; and building of the World Trade Bridge.

Flores' popularity dropped near the end of her term in 2005 with many issues on hand by the community. Some stated the deal with the proposed arena was a conflict because the land was owned by relatives of Flores and was supporting the arena development to her benefit. Also, discontent reached high when several dozen Laredo citizens went missing in Nuevo Laredo, Mexico and Flores claimed on national television these individuals were linked to the illegal drug traffic in some manner. This outraged the families of those involved including William Slemaker who had his stepdaughter missing and formed a group called Laredo's Missing. Slemaker was quoted in the Dallas News "whether she was involved or not, she wouldn't be the first one to have dated a drug trafficker," further stating, "that doesn't take the responsibility away from either government to investigate what happened to her."

Her popularity dropped as well when taxpayers saw city taxes increase dramatically during her tenure, which she had mentioned in a mayoral forum "I think we have to increase our taxes."

Several taxpayers were also angered for allowing the city to pay for liquor and a mariachi band for a celebration in Washington, D.C. Also, photos of several high-ranking Laredo officials, including former Police Chief Agustin Dovalina, Fire Chief Luis Sosa, Jr., and Health Department Director Hector Gonzalez drinking alcohol in a Washington D.C. trip were leaked.

In 2004, the city was sued over the use of credit cards by Mayor Betty Flores and City Manager Larry Dovalina. The lawsuit alleged the city failed to fully disclose the invoices of expenses from several credit cards used by Flores and Dovalina. The lawsuit claimed the city violated the provisions of the Freedom of Information Act and asked the court to order city officials not to use city credit cards for personal expenses and refrain from impairing the availability of government records.

The use of city-owned credit cards was much controversy in the Flores administration. A 2004 report from city records showed Flores, the mayor spending approximately $30,000 in 2002 in the city-issued American Express Gold Corporate card and almost $22,000 in the year 2003.

Former City Manager Larry Dovalina spent close to $100,000 in this city-issued card in 2002 and close to $75,000 in 2003. Reports showed city officials charged almost $500,000 on the city-issued card in those two years. According to city officials, most of the charges went towards travel and lodging, meals, travel agency fees, and association fees.

Halfway through the former mayor's term, Flores had traveled to Washington D.C., Boston, New York, Miami, San Diego, and Mexico City. Flores defended her trips stating Laredo gained much from these trips and exposure to our city.

Records also showed expenses included $334 for forty alcoholic drinks purchased from the city manager's city-issued card. Mayor Flores also purchased close to $5,000 in promotional tickets and merchandise from the Laredo Arena for concerts, events, and hockey games, in which Flores defended as using the money for promotional purposes for our city and low-income children.

From 1994 through 2005, it was reported the City of Laredo was sued at least six times for not complying with state laws on the use of open records requests and open meetings. The lawsuits cost the city close to $140,000 in attorney fees from outside agencies and settlement costs.

In 2006, Flores was term-limited and could not run for re-election. The Laredo mayoral race for 2006 included several candidates with two councilmen, John Galo and Jose A. Valdez, Jr. Also, Raul Salinas a retired FBI agent announced his campaign for mayor. The race included five candidates, and ultimately a run-off took place between Salinas and Galo. Flores did not endorse Salinas.

A June 17, 2006, run-off showed Raul G. Salinas the victor receiving 53% (9,665) of the vote against Galo's 8,657 votes. Galo outspent Salinas significantly and spent almost half a million dollars. Salinas had a 27-year history employed by the federal government including his service as an FBI agent. His slogan stated, "Right man, right time" referring to the climate of crime at the time where people were concerned from a spillover of the crime occurring in Mexico. The people believed Laredo needed someone with a law enforcement background to run the city and it worked for Salinas.

He described himself as a political outsider during his campaign and called himself the "people's mayor" as he would often be seen all around town. Critics of the former mayor stated he was great for photo-ops but accused him for lack of spine to lead Laredo facing big-city problems and an emerging nationwide negative image towards the city.

Critics stated Salinas was more of a figurehead mayor than a leader and worked well in the weak-mayor form of government. During his tenure, the council appointed a new police chief – twice, one after Dovalina, the police chief at the time resigned from corruption charges and the other when the proceeded chief moved out-of-state.

Laredo was also in the spotlight on national television with Al Roker's produced *Bordertown: Laredo* highlighting the Laredo Police Department's Narcotics unit.

Salinas ran for re-election in 2010 and had four opponents, including Councilman Gene Belmares, who was previously a Republican county chair and Juan Ramirez who endorsed Galo in 2006. Councilman Jose A. Valdez, Jr. was also a candidate and had endorsed Salinas in the 2006 run-off against Galo.

Ramirez told the *Texas Tribune* when running for mayor that Salinas was trying to revert to the "*patron system*" of government, stating, "You were either in good with whoever was in power, or you didn't get anything. That was the control they had in Laredo" in days past, Ramirez said. "We are starting to see the pattern of another *patrón* here with Mr. Salinas."

Belmares spent close to $100,000 on the race for mayor, much more than the incumbent Salinas where he received 34% of the run-off vote and Salinas garnering 66% or 12,783 votes. Salinas' ex-wife thanked supporters and even *cañoneros* in an election night victory speech.

Salinas throughout his term as mayor spoke against a proposed border wall and fought for immigration reform.

He was quoted leaving office at the end of his term stating, "I should have done more to make sure that the reputation of our community was sustained, and that the people were respected." He also wished he had more time left in his term. Salinas ran unsuccessfully for Webb County treasurer in 2014 losing to the incumbent Delia Perales in a run-off election.

2014 saw a change of leadership as the race for Laredo Mayor saw seven candidates in the race. No run-off would take place this time around as an attorney and former Laredo College Board of Trustee, Pete Saenz, Jr. would win outright with 53% of the vote over council member Cindy Liendo and former Webb County Commissioner and KGNS TV newscaster Jerry Garza. Saenz ran a campaign against corruption along with Webb County Judge Tano Tijerina, a former baseball player for the Milwaukee Brewers franchise and a rancher.

As soon as Saenz took office, he underwent hair-follicle drug testing along with several other councilmen to prove to the community they are drug-free. Shortly after that city manager Carlos Villarreal announced to the council, he would retire, prompting the council to conduct a nationwide search for a new city manager. Saenz told the community, "It wants a new person that has no roots or ties to any particular group."

Many cited the election of Saenz as a referendum to remove Villarreal. The council ultimately chose Assistant City Manager Jesus "Chuy" Olivares for the position. Upon leaving office, Villarreal received a severance package totaling $603,503, which included 18 months of pay and unused annual and sick leave he had accumulated. The council had voted earlier that year to give Villarreal a $40,000 annual raise. As his term in office progressed as mayor, Saenz faced much criticism by his fellow council members. The council was divided with the mayor on several issues about the city. He often used his veto power unsuccessfully over the council on several issues.

The division was seen when in a city council meeting former Councilman Roque Vela, Jr. was in a discussion with an individual, when Mayor Saenz told him "let him answer please, councilman." Vela then told Saenz, "sir, my mic is on, and I'm in a discussion with this man," to which Saenz replied knocking his gavel "and I'm the chair here, you're out of order." Vela said, "…and I'm the councilman that is sitting next to you, I think you're out of order Mayor." Vela continued with his discussion, and Saenz knocked his gavel again, stating, "You don't have the right to speak, he's got the right to speak at this point." Further saying, yes, "I am, I'm the mayor, I'm the chair! When you're here in this chair, you make that decision." Saenz referring to Vela stating the mayor was making unilateral decisions.

Vela mentioned how this "was a buildup" to what was to come and stated the mayor often interrupted during council meetings, stating, "We had to pay someone to show him how to run a meeting" referring to Roberts Rules of Orders.

Often time in contentious issues and contracts, many referred to the divided council as the "gang of five," where certain councilmen would vote for or against each other's agendas and issues.

Vela stated after his loss for reelection that Saenz "went there pounding his fists on the table, talking about how it's gonna be his way or the highway" and never really tried to get into the fold of things. Further stating, "He paints himself as one person in the public eye, and then you see what's really going on, and it's hard to get behind somebody like that."

In 2016, Saenz publicly endorsed a group named, Moving Laredo Forward and its charter initiatives. The charter initiatives had five charter changes, one changing the landscape of the political outlook of the city to have a hybrid system of four at-large districts and four divided districts, instead of the eight council districts. Other initiatives of the group supported providing more power to the mayor. The charter initiatives were on the ballot in November of 2016, and three of the five charter propositions passed, including one to allow the mayor to add items to council agendas and another to allow the mayor to initiate motions at council meetings. The majority of the council opposed the propositions and passed a resolution earlier that year.

Criticism from a local social media freelance reporter named, "*LaGordiloca*" arose when she stated Saenz was not as involved with the people as Mayor Salinas was and called for a recall petition of the mayor, which never evolved.

Some questioned the involvement of large developers receiving city contracts some who donated to the mayor and several city council campaigns or funded the city's Washington D.C. trip in 2015 and 2016. Saenz cited a healthy fund balance for the city and bringing in more businesses to Laredo to help create jobs. In his 2016 State of the

City address, Saenz stated, "We are poised for significant growth. We are galloping forward and catapulting Laredo to the next level."

The city election of 2016 saw the election of Nelly Vielma, an immigration attorney elected to the city council unseating Roque Vela, Jr. Mayor Saenz publicly supported Vielma. Opponents of Vielma argued she received large contributions from contractors and developers as such, as the Killam's and feared she would side with the other group of the council. Vela said he was surprised by the loss and initially thought it would have been a "long shot" to get defeated. He said he did not think he lost because he was a "bad councilmember, but as a matter of fact I think I lost because I was pretty damn effective" and "rubbed people the wrong way."

He mentioned in a radio program months later; he lost reelection because he got in the way of a developer, Cliffe Killam and partners who wanted 90 million dollars from a Tax Increment Reinvestment Zone (TIRZ) by the city in which he voted against. Vela stated, "In their eyes, I was the only reason they didn't get it because I rallied the votes and campaigned against it for months." He believed Killam was asking for too much money and did not vote against it because of whom they were or if the developments warranted. Vela told radio host Jay St. John, "there was one time when we (Cliffe Killam and Vela) were sitting in a conference room at the bowling alley, and he was pulling his hair out and couldn't understand why I wouldn't just vote for it… he sits back and goes, you know I'm gonna get what I want one way or another right?" Vela has stated Vielma; his opponent was number five or six of the people who "they" spoke to run against him in the election because no one wanted to run against him. He also mentioned Mayor Saenz "was involved in looking for a candidate to run against" him.

In a run-off election in December, outgoing Councilman Juan Narvaez was term-limited, and Webb County Democratic chair Alberto Torres won the election with 56.44% of the vote compared to his challenger, Laredo College Board Vice-President Allen Tijerina's 43.56%. Narvaez supported Torres in his campaign. Tijerina had received the majority of the votes in the November election. Torres stayed as Democrtic County Chair and councilman.

Shortly after the new council, in April of 2017, the Federal Bureau of Investigations raided several local public offices and the offices of Dannenbaum Engineering. The FBI seized records from City Hall and county offices pertaining to dealings with the engineering company. All sitting councilmembers were the subject of FBI lists, which included four councilmen in a target list and another four council members in a secondary list. The target list also included City Manager Jesus "Chuy" Olivares. As a result, Mayor Saenz called for the city manager to be placed on paid suspension, as he was the subject of the FBI's target-list. Olivares said placing this item on the agenda was unreasonable. On May 15, 2017, after an executive session at city council, Olivares announced to the council he would be retiring. Saenz wished him well and was satisfied with the outcome. The council ultimately chose assistant city manager Horacio De Leon who would be making $9,000 more than Olivares plus a $1,200 monthly car allowance for a yearly salary of $276,200 a year.

The 2018 municipal elections saw two councilmen termed out, including Alex Perez and Charlie San Miguel. San Miguel unsuccessfully ran for mayor finishing third behind the incumbent, Saenz and former councilman Roque Vela, Jr. who were both in a run-off election. Vela faced history where there had not been an incumbent mayor defeated in the past decades in Laredo and Saenz ultimately won re-election with 64% of the vote. Dr. Marte Martinez won in a runoff election race against activist Vish Viswanath after facing an unprecedented eleven candidates in the open seat. Mercurio "Merc" Martinez III, the son of Mercurio Martinez, Jr. won the district three council race after facing the incumbent's wife Crissy Perez in the runoff.

In what was the first meeting of 2019 and of the newly elected council members, City Manager Horacio De Leon announced his retirement. City council spent the night of January 22nd behind closed doors in executive session where they discussed De Leon's performance after approving the city manager's employment agreement just several months before. De Leon had only served as city manager for less than two years and had been the city's third city manager in just under four years. Council expressed an interest in seeking a city manager from out of town.

In October of 2019, council voted to receive their own retirement benefits. A city spokesman said the retirement benefits is mandatory according to the Texas Municipal Retirement System Act as elected officials who work more than 1,000 hours a year should be considered city employees and eligible to participate in the retirement system. Council took action to adopt the ordinance where the city will match retirement contributions up to 7% at a rate of 2:1. Mayor Saenz said each council member would have to answer to the public whether they will participate, but said he justifies his participation, as he being mayor is a full-time job.

As of 2019, council members make $50,000 a year and the mayor $75,000, which includes cellphone, vehicle, and office allowances.

Chapter 5:

THE SECOND MINI REVOLUTION

In the mid-1990's Laredo City Hall was shaken up by several newly elected council members. Texas Monthly called it the conservative revolt and led by former Councilman for district two, Louis H. Bruni. Of course, Bruni's uncle was the former mayor; you guessed it, JC Martin, Jr. He stated his father was also part of the old Independent Club and wanted to undo this so-called "family feud" from his name once and for all.

Bruni was elected into the Laredo city council in 1994 and re-elected in 1998 by only sixty-four votes defeating Mercurio Martinez III, son of Mercurio Martinez, Jr. who Bruni would unseat in 2002 for Webb County Judge.

He led the charge for a different council and gathered a temporary conservative governing majority in the city council. After his 1994 election, the city saw the election of council members Alfonso "Poncho" Casso, Consuelo "Chelo" Montalvo, Mario Alvarado, and Republican gas station owner Joe Guerra. Guerra previously served under the Martin administration but was not part of the Old Party.

With the election of these individuals, the city council and Bruni finally had a majority (five) that made major changes within city government not seen since the election of Aldo Tatangelo.

In the several weeks preceding their election victories, the council voted to fire former City Manager Peter Vargas and accepted the resignation of then-Assistant City Manager Carlos Villarreal who then became City Manager in 2007. They also demoted Police Chief J.L. Martinez, the city attorney, and head of convention and visitor's bureau. The directors of parks and recreation, utilities, and transportation departments were re-assigned or resigned.

Bruni called Carlos Villarreal in 1996 "the secret conduit to the ex-mayor and his cronies." However, Villarreal was later hired as Executive Administrator to the commissioner's court in 2003 under Bruni as Webb County judge. He was quoted in a *Laredo Morning Times* article, he would "consider (Villarreal) a complement to the court of which (he is) a member," but he would not let the new hire "interfere with (his) staff."

As a county judge, Bruni was unhappy with former commissioner Jerry Vasquez as he felt he was disparaging his staff for wanting Villarreal. In 2004, Bruni's Bailiff Frank Sciaraffa ran against Vasquez and won the seat. He sued Sciaraffa, a one-time ally of Bruni for alleged non-payment of loans and interest. Bruni ran against him in 2012 and 2016 for the commissioner's seat unsuccessfully.

On January 14, 2004, Alfonso "Poncho" Casso another one-time ally of Bruni called for his removal as Webb County Judge due to what Casso called as alleged actions and behavior the judge exhibited as an elected official. Bruni lost re-election in 2006 against former Justice of the Peace Danny Valdez.

During the time of the 90's so-called conservative revolt, Casso attempted to run for mayor in 1998 but lost the election to Betty Flores. He lived across the street from where Bruni resided and launched his campaign for city council as Bruni encouraged him. He would write to the local newspaper and speak out against then Mayor Saul Ramirez.

Legend has it Casso and Ramirez became so heated that the ex-mayor kicked him. The brawls such resembled nearly those of the *"Botas"* and *"Guaraches."* Casso told Texas Monthly in 1996 "A bunch of times we had to be physically separated." Referring to him and Ramirez.

Many residents at the time turned on their televisions to the public access channel to watch the live city council meetings as it were primetime Sunday Night Football. Casso publicly stated he was the only one with the "balls" to run in Laredo and stated in a Pro 8 News recap of the mayoral race he was running for mayor "not just to cut ribbons" but do more than that if elected.

At one time, there was an alleged murder plot against Casso, like a plot straight out of the old feuds. The councilman looked into bringing federal obstruction of justice charges against former District Attorney Joe Rubio from a case involving a high-profile triple-ax murder case in 1991. Casso was determined to investigate the police and the district attorney's office. Casso said, "We found out that basically the police department was just doing a lousy job on the way they handled evidence and stored evidence and the way they were transferred to the DA's office." He believed it was a cover-up to protect certain people such as in the triple ax homicide, saying, "The best thing to do is to destroy fingerprints and lose them."

In some would call a retaliatory manner, the District Attorney arrested Casso for a technical violation of the Texas Open Meetings Act and charges were later not pursued. Some claim Rubio succeeded in destroying Casso's political career, but Casso says his investigation grew interest from the FBI and any investigation may not have occurred without him looking into it.

Regarding city hall at this time, those involved with the majority council stated these council members were a breath of fresh air much like when Tatangelo was elected mayor.

The councilmembers of this short-lived era eventually moved on from their positions. Bruni was elected Webb County judge and the other candidates went away due to term limits, retirements, or lost elections.

Chapter 6:

FAMILY TIES

We all know it is mostly all in the family but in politics, this runs grand especially in Laredo politics. Some say it is good and some argue otherwise saying it may lead to corruption or dynasties. Since the dismantlement of the *Partido Viejo*, which many argue is still alive and well, many family members have been elected to serve by the voters in various capacities.

The mayorship of Laredo was controlled by one family tree for generations. The founder of Laredo, Captain Tomas Sanchez was the first, a great, great, great grandfather to Tirza Garcia, maternal grandmother to JC Martin, Jr. Other relatives who served as mayor were Santiago Sanchez, Tomas Antonio Sanchez, Basilio Benavides, Santos Benavides, Refugio Benavides, Juan Francisco Farias, Rosendo Garcia, Julian Garcia, and Albert Martin. Bartolo Garcia, Tirza Garcia's father also served as mayor circa 1854.

The bloodlines run deep and even in politics, one cannot deny how strong their urge to serve is. One can make their judgment on whether any of the proceedings were or are corrupt, but the bloodlines do not lie and well, it is what it is. To understand the current family ties of modern elected officials we must look into the past, the Old Party's past.

In the early to mid-1900's eighty five percent of Laredoans were Mexican American, and most of the Anglo-Saxon race in Laredo were tied to the Old Party directly or through marriage. Some recognizable names that still ring today are the Leyendeckers, Sames, Maddox, Haynes, Valls, and Summers.

Joseph Claude Martin, Jr. (JC Martin, Jr.) was mayor of Laredo and served on the 49th district judicial clerk, he is the son of JC Martin, Sr., who served a Webb County sheriff and president of the Laredo Independent School District. Raymond Martin, the leader of the *Botas*, is the father of Martin Sr. and grandfather to the ex-mayor. Antonio M. Bruni is the son of Raymond Martin who served as Webb County treasurer and Webb County commissioner. Honore Ligarde is the brother-in-law to JC Martin, Jr. and served as a Texas state representative and Webb County commissioner. Albert Martin is an uncle of Martin, Jr., who served as mayor of Laredo in the 1920's. Billy Hall, Jr great grandfather was Antonio M. Bruni; Hall served as a state representative and Webb County treasurer. Louis H. Bruni is the nephew of Martin, Jr. and served as Laredo city councilman and Webb County judge. John C. Galo has a brother married to JC Martin's daughter and served as Laredo city councilman and Webb County commissioner.

We cannot forgo speaking of family ties without mentioning the Kazen's. The Kazen family was second to the Martin's in having as many members in key local political positions. At one point in time, there as E. James Kazen as a district attorney, O.H. Kazen as a county clerk, and Abraham Kazen as a state representative serving from

1947 through 1953, state senator from 1953 through 1967, and in the U.S. Congress from 1967 through 1985.

The Kazen's also had M.J. Raymond who was a brother-in-law to Abraham Kazen and served as the Webb County Democratic Chairman. Later in 1979 President Jimmy Carter appointed George P. Kazen, an uncle of Abraham Kazen as U.S. District Court Judge.

Many argue the dynasties of families are still rampant within our elected and appointed public offices. The Cuellar's have had three public offices occupied, including the United States Congress with Henry Cuellar, the Webb County sheriff's department with Martin Cuellar, and the Laredo Municipal Court Judge and Tax Assessor Collector with Rosie Cuellar – all siblings of the Cuellar family.

The Webb County Courthouse has two relatives in the elected office chairs. Webb County Judge Tano Tijerina is Webb County Commissioner Rosaura "Wawi" Tijerina's aunt by marriage. County Judge Tijerina was quoted in the Texas Tribune stating, "My family is the backbone, but that's not the only bone… I don't see how it's just the border" referring to his relation to the county commissioner.

Former Webb County Justice of the Peace Ricardo Rangel who served from 2002 through 2014 is the uncle of former council member and LC trustee Esteban Rangel. The former justice of the peace is also the brother-in-law to former Justice of the Peace Ramiro Veliz, Jr. The former Webb County Justice of the Peace Ramiro Veliz, Jr. who was first elected in 2006 is the father of United Independent School District Board Trustee, Ramiro Veliz III elected in 2012.

Webb County Justice of the Peace Hector Liendo who was first elected in 1992 is the brother of another Justice of the Peace, Oscar Liendo, elected in 2006. Cindy Liendo, Hector Liendo's daughter, served in the Laredo city council from 2008 through 2015 and unsuccessfully ran for mayor, then ran successfully for Laredo ISD trustee. Cindy Linedo was elected county commissioner in 2018.

Former Laredo City Councilman Jose A. Valdez, Jr. who ran for mayor unsuccessfully in 2006 and 2010 and the Laredo City Secretary is the son of former City Councilman and Laredo ISD Board of Trustee Jose A. Valdez.

Mayor Pete Saenz, Jr. is related by marriage to former County Judge Mercurio Martinez, Jr. and Councilman Mercurio "Merc" Martinez III.

Former County Court at Law II Judge Jesus "Chuy" Garza is the brother of Ricardo Garza, an LISD board of trustee.

Councilman Rodolfo "Rudy" Gonzalez is a cousin to County Commissioner Jesse Gonzalez.

49th District Court Judge Joe Lopez is the brother-in-law to former Councilman Alex Perez.

State Senator Judith Zaffirini's brother-in-law was Charles Borchers who served as District Attorney from 1973 through 1980.

Former City Manager Larry Dovalina who served from 2000 through 2006 is a cousin to Agustin Dovalina, the former Laredo police chief, and Ramon H. Dovalina, who served as Laredo Community College president from 1995 through 2007.

Webb County Attorney Marco Montemayor is a brother to United Independent School District Board of Trustee Javier Montemayor, Jr.

Porfirio Lauro Flores, a former Webb County Sheriff, unseated by Mario Santos in 1976 was the father-in-law to Julio A. Garcia, a former District Attorney for Webb and Zapata counties who served from 1981 through 1988. Garcia is also a distant relative to former District Attorney Joe Rubio who succeeded him in 1988.

Former District Attorney Joe Rubio is a maternal cousin of Texas State Representative Richard Raymond.

Chapter 7:

"CORRUPTION" IN POLITICS

"The person who is trustworthy in very small matters is also trustworthy in great ones" - Luke 16:10

As written previously, our community has seen numerous elected and public officials resign, arrested, and convicted of corruption charges. One can argue if corruption includes those who commit crimes or just those about the office they serve. In any matter, according to Merriam-Webster, corruption is defined as an "impairment of integrity, virtue, or moral principle… inducement to wrong by improper or unlawful means (as bribery), or a departure from the original or from what is pure or correct."

At any rate, corruption is corruption, and any elected or public official should be held to the highest standard. There should be no room for intimidation or bribery; an elected office is in place to serve the people solely, as it is theirs.

There is also the usual politics involved in which I consider several terms that could be placed. Political recycling is when an elected official runs for another office, thus seeking votes and applause from constituents to win another election. I also coined the term political defriending, much like on social media when someone "unfriends" a person on their Facebook, this happens in politics too. You see "political defriending" occurs when two or more candidates or elected officials were united in voting and running together, and then suddenly disband when there is a disagreement or feud happens.

We also see the term political padrino/compadre/boss; this is used when an elected official or politician wanna-be runs the show at a certain government entity, be it in the city, county, or schools.

Political grandstanding is also used to coin when a politician is seen everywhere an event occurs to gain attention or name recognition to obtain votes or praise. They often attempt to take credit for something they had little or nothing to do but happen to be in the spotlight of such occurrence for their convenience politically.

Political concealing is a term I coined to call those candidates and elected officials who participate in an award they are issued when they are in the midst of running for reelection or a campaign. This usually happens when a local organization "honors" a certain politico for their "efforts" in the community and creates a "fandango" and press releases to expose this particular politician in a "positive" manner, thus gaining attention from the voters – often free advertising or exposure.

We also see the word political machine, in which there is a group of people running certain candidates and or elected officials, an antonym of political defriending. This could be a particular area of town where candidates merge into groups wanting control of several elected offices in the city, county, and schools. They crave the power of certain seats in parts of town from various elected offices, much like a quasi-mafia.

We also have politicians who are just plain lazy. A former council member said the majority of the council members try to get their work done at the council meeting, show up unprepared, and not do what is needed in between the meetings. They just show up to vote and take the credit – making it all smoke and mirrors to their constituents. An opposite of what it is to serve the community.

Back to true corruption, an *Express-News Rio Grande Valley* article titled "Laredo residents silent on corruption" was published on November 3, 2007, mentioning how "Most everyone has a brother, a cousin — someone in the family — who works for the city, the county, the school board, or U.S. Customs and Border Protection. People fear that speaking out will risk that someone's livelihood."

Basically, it is our duty as members of the community to stay silent on corruption when we hear it, more like a tradition or way of life, which is no longer surprising or eye-popping. The norm continues, as corruption has been a way of life for Webb County since its dawn of day and continues to be.

A gas station business owner mentioned in the article stating, "It's basically keep your mouth shut, keep your job."

Former Webb County Sheriff Rick Flores was quoted in responding to Chief Augustin Dovalina's case and corruption stating, "It gets to the point where you become complacent, you become careless. And when you become careless, you're going to make mistakes," Flores said, " You also need to surround yourself with good people. Corruption doesn't only exist in local law enforcement; corruption exists in every agency in law enforcement."

Often times you hear people in the community mention how a college degree or experience does not matter here because it is mostly "who you know, not what you know," when obtaining a job particularly in the city, county, or schools.

One can easily check public records and find there are children of a councilman serving as firefighters or relatives of public officials serving in the county jail or a high paying city office. Whether these individuals got the position because they truly were the best qualified is truly nothing to prove in most cases.

A "Democrat" Webb County?

While Webb County is mostly Democrat, some say this is not truly the case, and rather we have one form of government party not belonging to any affiliation of Democrats or Republicans. Congressman Henry Cuellar who represents Laredo in the United States Congress votes many times with his Republican counterparts on issues in this so-called strong Democratic stronghold. In 2019, a liberal group names Justice Democrats announced they were going to challenge Cuellar in a primary because of his voting record and fundraising support of GOP candidates. The congressman's voting record is more conservative than the majority of other House Democrat's and voted 70 percent with President Trump. Some candidates who run in a Democratic primary are not truly Democrats if you look into their political contributions. A candidate for mayor had donated to state Republican candidates, another candidate for county judge donated only to GOP candidates. However, one can argue if anyone wants a true shot to win an election in Webb County, running as a Republican in their primary would automatically mean you lost your election as only a small portion in Webb County vote Republican.

On the other hand, while Webb County has seen a decreasing number of Republican candidates running in elections, a slowly growing number of Green Party candidates had emerged in a period of time. In 2014, we saw Green Party candidate Erika Martinez, a candidate for Webb County Commissioner received 42.78% against the Democratic Party chosen candidate, Frank Sciaraffa. Lakshmana "Vish" Viswanath, a Green Party candidate for Webb County justice of the peace, saw him receive 25.48% of the vote against the Democratic opponent, Jose "Pepe" Salinas in the general election. Supporters of the Green Party say this is a sign of people wanting a choice other than just an unopposed candidate in a Democratic Party candidate. Green Party candidates faded by 2018 and saw an emergence of republican candidates challenging local Democrats on the ballot. Former city councilman Poncho Casso ran against incumbent County Judge Tano Tijerina and garnered 24% of the vote. Representative Richard Raymond also saw a challenge from a Republican with Luis De La Garza earning 26% of the vote.

Employment in City & County

We have seen corruption in the community of Laredo and Webb County in all aspects of government – city, county, courts, and schools. Some cases have gone unnoticed while others have been prosecuted in a court of law. Often time, the corrupt acts of an elected or public official go noticed in a court of public opinion but rather than replacing the individual in a re-election, they elect them for another term. We cannot award corrupt individuals any more terms in office and must take responsibility for ourselves to protect our precious community from the corrupt tactics of our officials, be it legal or not; corruption is corruption. Many fear corruption in Webb County is a way of life.

In a 2004 report, employees who had sued Webb County for wrongful termination were paid more than $339,137.33 in settlements, all coming from your taxpayer money and most of these positions coming from those elected to office. We have seen many times when employees under an elected official have their jobs terminated left with unemployment once a newly elected individual takes their seat. People employed under elected officials, as their boss are often worried when a change occurs in election season because their job is uncertain. Even now where civil service is in place, employees are not assured.

An instance was in December of 2002 when a newly elected Webb County clerk having not yet taken office at this time sent a letter to sixteen employees from this department stating their services were no longer needed once this official took office. A leaked memo on December 9, 2002, stated, "This is to inform you that I, will not be able to hire you as I, begin my term of office as Webb County Clerk on January 1, 2003. Sincerely, Margie Ramirez Ibarra."

Ibarra was the newly elected county clerk at the time and has won re-election since. She told the media she was not firing anyone, but just not hiring anyone back.

"I'm not firing because I'm not the county clerk at the present time," she said. "When I take over, I will be hiring whoever is coming in with me," Ibarra told the media.

In March of 2005, the county attorney advised former Sheriff Rick Flores that the employment of two relatives was against the law. The former sheriff had two brothers-in-laws, including Cayetano Tijerina, also a relative of Webb County Judge to be Tano Tijerina, employed and had to be removed. Flores told the media, "It is my position as a sworn public servant to do the right thing and I have done just that, and I will continue to do so." According to state law, an official cannot appoint an individual to a position compensated with public funds if the person is related to the official within three degrees of blood relations or two degrees of marriage.

We often hear of people running for elected office promising positions to those who support them, thus having a job waiting for them there once they win their elected office. Do you wonder why often time how enthusiastic a voter can be for supporting a candidate? This is rampant in those campaigns for office where elected officials hire and fire and have the highest paying jobs in our community. Of course, one will help a candidate if they are offered a good paying job at the county, city, or school. Not saying all of our enthusiastic supporters of democracy are in it for this, some are relatives, friends, and just supporters of their issues, but do you think this is mostly the case? One knows it is election season when they see a bunch of people rally in street corners holding signs and yelling the name of their candidate. Some as stated are just friends, family or supporters of the candidate, but some are also in it for their gain. Others are paid by a candidate to stand in for them and campaign rally in these sidewalks, some being illegal aliens. Those candidates with the most money to spend in campaigns are often the ones who can afford to buy people to support them other than offering them something for gain once elected. Democracy, economics, or just plain corrupted. You decide.

Employees under the sheriff's department have also seen their share of unemployment once an incumbent sheriff loses re-election. From 2013 throughout, we saw the rise of an activist posting YouTube videos exposing some of the wrongdoings, corruption, or unethical occurrences at the Webb County jail and within the sheriff's department. Some argue this is not the case, but the facts speak for themselves.

A Webb County jail captain hired by Sheriff Martin Cuellar in April of 2015 who had skipped the rank of corporal and lieutenant was a fast food restaurant manager just seven years earlier. This individual went from corporal to sergeant, then a captain in this span of years. Some stated others were highly qualified who had more experience and had qualifications as peace officers and other credentials and training.

The activist stated he was hired by helping him his political campaigns, including Cuellar's sister's municipal court judge campaign.

Other YouTube videos by the activist show there are allegations of nepotism, manipulation of official documents, deceptive hiring practices, and other corruption at the sheriff's department.

Pay increases for elected officials

Elected officials also often argue and ask for an increase in their salary. Many of these elected positions are highly paid, such as those in the Webb County commissioner's court, justice of the peace, and constables averaging $75,000 per year. A justice of the peace in Texas does not require anyone holding the office to have experience or degree in law and just needs to be elected.

In 2013, the Webb County commissioner's court approved a 2.5% hike for all elected officials, yes elected officials. The sheriff already made more than $130,000 a year, while a constable in Precinct 1 made over $77,000 a year. In September of 2014, Constable Rudy Rodriguez fought the commissioner's court for having them taken away a $12,000 stipend granted only to him. The other three constables made less than he did, and the commissioner's court eventually voted to deny an increase for the other three constables and leave the $12,000 stipend for Rodriguez. This move was made because the $12,000 stipend was for a mental health unit his office had, which was moved to the sheriff's department. Rodriguez kept the stipend after this action, and he took it to the salary grievance committee and won.

Webb County Commissioners contemplated on voting for pay raises for all county-elected official again in the summer of 2019. A proposal was originally voted on to give a $20,500 raise to the county judge and $17,600 yearly raise to county commissioners. The proposal came after the county paid a consulting firm for a study of salaries of elected officials. Commissioner Jesse Gonzalez said the pay increases were needed because there had not been any raises in years and if the county waited any longer, the situation would get worse. After weeks of public backlash, the country ultimately voted down the raises.

While most elected officials make a lot of money from our taxes, some still managed to crave even more out of greed, be it an increase in salary, contributions, or even shady dealings.

An employee under a former Webb County justice of the peace one stated to me; the judge was seen getting cash from a marriage fee he presided. The former justice of the peace allegedly took the fee in cash and said a prayer before placing his money in the pocket to use for recreation in "*las maquinitas*."

Misuse of power?

The Webb County's Community Action Agency was raided by the FBI in 2011 and found employees who had allegedly misused state-funded weatherization for homes to those who did not qualify for the assistance. Former County Judge Andres Ramos was one of the individuals benefiting in receiving funds from this agency. As a result, the CAA was suspended in 2010 and Webb County fired twenty-six employees. In 2017, the FBI concluded there was no wrongdoing and found no evidence of losing federal programs funds to this.

On another unrelated county issue, October of 2013 saw the Webb County Attorney investigating Commissioner Rosaura "Wawi" Tijerina with a possible violation of the state nepotisms law by voting to transfer her sister-in-law to a higher position in 2012. Tijerina seconded a motion in a May 2012 commissioner's court meeting where the motion was in place to promote her relative to a secretarial position from a part-time job.

A further meeting in December of 2012, Tijerina made a motion to promote the relative from the current position to a multi-agency specialist, thus increasing the pay from $14.35 an hour to $16.89 an hour. The agenda items did not mention the name of the employee to be promoted and only their job titles and hourly pay.

Tijerina told the media, "If the agenda didn't mention her name, then I didn't know she was going to receive a promotion." She stated she abstained in past agenda items if she knew whom the item pertained to. She further mentioned, her sister-in-law was hired on her own merits and had nothing to do with the interview or supervising and had nothing to hide. In two years, Tijerina's sister-in-law went from a part-time employee to a multi-agency specialist earning more than $20 an hour.

The city council also faced their battles in nepotism when on October of 2012 a lawsuit was filed by a resident through his attorney, Sergio "Keko" Martinez claiming city councilman Charlie San Miguel violated the Laredo City Charter when his two twin sons were hired as firefighters by the City of Laredo. San Miguel argued firefighters are exempt from the anti-nepotism section of the city charter because the city has a civil service commission. Members of the community, including VIDA (Voices in Democratic Action), a watchdog group claimed there was also a conflict with the city's attorney representing the councilman because Raul Casso, the city attorney at the time had a brother who is the owner of Rapidos Transfer who had a contract awarded to him by the city along with Garros who is owned by San Miguel's sister along with Eduardo Garza (owner of Uni-Trade).

A local resident claimed he knew one of the applicants who was next on the list but this person was never advised of the status of the application, saying, "He later found out that he was cut from the list due to all the positions have been filled."

Casso released a statement stating the councilman's sons were not subject to the nepotism clause because firefighters' collective bargaining agreement with the city does not address nepotism. As a result, the city council voted unanimously to formally request a city council nepotism prohibition from the police and fire civil service commission in its civil service rules. San Miguel abstained in this vote.

Later in 2015, San Miguel introduced ethics training for city employees and was one of the four votes in 2017 on council stating a fellow councilman Vidal Rodriguez's actions in which he was guilty of was not considered moral turpitude.

Naming of parks and public buildings

The naming of parks and public buildings across Laredo are mostly named after has been politicians or sometimes if they are lucky, current ones such as in some Laredo ISD facilities.

However, in the strange case of a naming of a pool, we go back to the summer of 2013 where the City of Laredo opened a year-round pool in North Central Park. There were many controversies not because of the pool itself, but because of the name. Council member of district six, Charlie San Miguel had this pool set in his district, and the name of the pool was honored in the name of his parents, Rev. Deacon Leonel and Irma San Miguel. Many residents questioned if this was the right move by the city to name a pool after a sitting councilman's parents and a pool that is located in the district he serves.

Contributions to stay elected

Running a campaign can be expensive. Many candidates running for office spend far more than what they would receive in compensation if elected. For instance, a candidate for city council can and have spent over $100,000 running for a spot on the council and in compensation would receive about $50,000 a year. In September of 2016, council voted to increase their annual salary to $50,000 and the mayor to $75,000. Before this, the expense and compensation ratio were farther apart.

The same goes for a candidate running for commissioner, justice of the peace, constable, county judge, or a judge, although their annual salaries are higher. Corruption can stem from running these costly campaigns, and this is when contributions kick in. You see there is nothing illegal taking campaign contributions, and some receive monetary campaign contributions from donors who benefit from a "yes" vote at city council or the commissioner's court. One look at the financial reports of an incumbent running for re-election, one can see contributions from wealthy individuals in the oil, ranching, and city contracting business, reminiscent of the Martin days.

We cannot blame just the incumbents as a fresh candidate running for office are at times hand-picked by wealthy individuals to get them elected into office, so maybe, just maybe they'll benefit from their elected official status in more than just being their concerned citizen being listened to by their elected official.

One needs to be wary of what a writer, Mikaela Rodriguez once called "…a long line of mythic Robin Hood-esque *patróns*, big men who ran local politics by buying elections, putting friends and business partners on the city's payroll and serving as paternalistic figures for loyal voters."

No, she was not talking about the current political scene, but that of the JC "Pepe" Martin rule, however, one can surely relate this statement to today's view of politics in Webb County, a sad but heartfelt truth in our psyche. A former Laredoan and young activist John Castro once told the media "…the activists in town are too busy squabbling for the scraps off the table of big politicians. They're willing to lie, deceive and backstab to get it." Castro left Laredo after dissolving an organization he created in 2004 called Laredo Students in Democratic Action. The organization was developed to expose corruption by current elected officials at the time that included the mayor, city manager, council members, and the district attorney.

Lemurs closure

In May of 2017, Laredo saw baseball go away as the Laredo Lemurs were "forever lost" according to owner Arianna Torres. According to her attorney, she invested $2,600,000 in the franchise and stated she was the only funding option for the team. Torres filed a lawsuit against Marcus Holliman and Saul Villarreal, the Lemur's two other owners claiming they both mismanaged operations and attempted to sell the baseball team without her knowing. Both denied the allegations.

On April 28 of 2017, Judge Oscar Hale granted Torres control of the Laredo Lemurs. Torres stated the city would not approve of her plan outlined by Judge Hale after she was granted control. She stated, "The season did not happen because the city refused to allow the changes necessary to give the Lemurs its only hope to be a successful organization." Torres said her dream of owning a sports team quickly turned into a nightmare and "due completely to the City's bizarre insistence that I hire two people it recommended to manage the operation. From day one they were a cancer on the organization that prevented any shot whatsoever of success." She further claimed in what she called the other two owners "The Management Duo" were threatening her "acting with authority and on behalf of the City Manager."

2015 documents reveal that the City of Laredo also has a recycling contract with Villarreal and Holliman. Critics argued this was a conflict of interest as Villarreal was also associated with the Laredo Development Foundation, which receives third party funding by the city. Holliman was a member of the local appraisal board and appointed by former Councilman Juan Narvaez to the Economic Development Advisory Committee.

Torres told the public these two individuals did not have the experience to run the sports team and wanted to bring in a partner with experience but the city "wanted a deal where their two favored characters ran the show or no deal at all. That's why it all fell apart." Later in 2017, Laredo also learned they would not see the Laredo Swarm, a basketball team from the ABA return. One of the owners mentioned the city did not want to pay anymore for the team to stay in Laredo and could not come to terms with the city on the arena they played in.

On May 8 of 2017, the Laredo City Council voted to have the Lemurs vacate the premises of the UniTrade Stadium and set out proposals for buyers or leasers for the stadium. In 2018, baseball returned to Laredo as the city agreed to bring the Tecolotes, a baseball team from the Mexican League of Professional Baseball to the UniTrade Stadium.

Chapter 8:

CORRUPTION AND UNETHICAL CASES

Ethical dilemmas have a way of sneaking up on a person. If something smells funny, stay away from it. Or help get rid of it. –Prince Pritchett

The city of Laredo and its surrounding area has seen its share of unethical cases and corruption from public officials throughout the years after the Old Party rule. The line of what is ethical and not is set by the voters, the public, and democracy, and or the law.

Important to note those mentioned in the writing are individuals, some who have contributed much to our community positively and cannot in totality take away the negativity in the events that have occurred.

Triple axe Smiley case

Jose Marcellno Rubio, Jr. served as district attorney for Webb and Zapata counties from 1989 through 2008. A high-profile murder case in Laredo in early 1991 had implications for Rubio. The triple-axe murder case as it is known involved a murder by two teens in the north Laredo home of James D. Smiley, 33 in the 900 block of Carrol Drive. The knives and axe used in the murders were provided to the killers by Manuel "Milo" Flores, the son of former District Judge Manuel R. Flores. His son was also the gateway driver.

In this corruption case, Rubio was accused of failing to procure an indictment against Flores' son. People argued this was because of the political ties between Flores, his father, and the district attorney. The ex-wife of Flores testified under oath in late 1996 on the notion that Rubio and Flores held an illegal meeting to protect Milo Flores from prosecution. Rubio denied having to participate in a meeting with Manuel Flores under oath days after her testimony.

In a 2018 interview on a Netflix program called "*I Am a Killer*", former District Court Judge Manuel Flores acknowledged that the group of teens, including the two teens who murdered Smiley were together at his home and that his son had given them a ride into the neighborhood where they committed the murders. Flores said, he would have preferred his son to be accused, "and face a jury of his peers and that he would've been declared innocent," saying "because there were no facts that showed any guilt."

Another alleged case of corruption involved Rubio's father, Jose Marcelino "Pichino" Rubio, Sr. In the spring of 2000, Rubio's father was found guilty of conspiracy and extortion. This case occurred after a federal sweep was conducted by the district attorney's office in 1997 and Rubio's father and four other people, including prosecutors and a judge, were convicted of charges involving case fixing. Evidence could not link the district attorney to the case when his father made a motion requesting to be home confined in 2003. His father was present in the district attorney's office daily, but no evidence suggested a link to take bribes for a favorable action in his case.

His father was released in November of 2006 after over three years of confinement. Another case involving Rubio's brother involved a case-fixing violation, which included district attorney's office employees. He was sentenced to thirty-two months in a federal prison in 2000 and released in August of 2002. The case also implicated an uncle and cousin of Rubio. Rubio decided not to seek reelection in 2008 and was replaced by Isidro "Chilo" Alaniz, a former assistant district attorney under Rubio.

City Secretary sexual harassment

Gustavo Guevara was Laredo's city secretary for almost thirty years. The position of city secretary was formally an elected position. In 2006, a lawsuit was filed against the City of Laredo. Hilda Negrete, an employee who worked under Guevara who was her supervisor at the time, brought the lawsuit forth. She claimed Guevara sexually harassed her while working, and eventually a jury awarded her half a million dollars in damages plus $200,000 in attorney fees. Negrete's sworn complaint against Guevara alleged he made unwelcome advances to her; called her after hours inviting her to dinner; created an unflattering image of her; sent two arrangements of roses to her office; and displayed a pornographic image to other city officials on his office computer.

Guevara also allegedly told her she was beautiful and implied he wanted to say something personal to her during a phone conference in the presence of co-workers.

Guevara remained in his position and was not fired; he was only suspended for thirty days without pay and had to attend sexual harassment training. He retired in late 2015.

Drugs and politics

One thing people and the media fascinate about is drugs, rock and roll and politics. District seven Councilman Jorge A. Vera was arrested in July 2014 at a local rock music bar in the early morning hours. It is what followed from public outcry that created a recall for him by a local attorney who eventually took over his seat.

Vera was indicted that month for cocaine possession and making a false report to a peace officer. He was at a local bar; AJ's Bar in north Laredo when he allegedly offered a woman cocaine and told her he had some in his truck. The woman called police and Vera's truck was searched by Laredo Police officers where they found an illegal substance in his vehicle. Also arrested in this matter was Jose Degollado, a relative of Esther Degollado, a Webb County Clerk and employee for the District Attorney's office for tampering with evidence.

The councilman called a police department official and another fellow councilman while in custody of the peace officers in the wee hours of the morning from his cell phone.

Vera told the media and the police his truck was broken into and as he was questioned, the former councilman was released.

He attended a council meeting at City Hall that evening within hours of the incident. Vera turned himself in later that week as an arrest warrant was issued by District Judge Oscar Hale.

Attorney and activist George Altgelt wanted Vera removed from his post and successfully gathered enough signatures from the voters of the district to call for a recall of the councilman. A recall election took place on November 2014, and the voters decided to recall Vera, thus creating a vacancy. A special election was held in early 2015 where Altgelt entered the open race and won taking over the seat Vera previously held.

Vera was the first city official to be removed from office through a recall petition.

Dirty water

Former Laredo City Councilman Johnny Amaya who was term-limited and left the council in 2008 became a Laredo Independent School District board trustee in 2010 and worked as a systems manager with the Webb County utilities department.

He was arrested in 2014 for allegedly tampering government paperwork regarding a Rio Bravo, Texas and El Cenizo, Texas water system scandal, in which caused residents of this small community to boil their water for several weeks as traces of E. Coli were found in their water supply.

The district attorney indicted Amaya and seven other employees as the Texas Rangers discovered tampering of daily and monthly reports with false figures of turbidity endangering its residents. Allegedly, Amaya ordered the documents to be tampered by his supervisors and employees. The 111th District Court was presented with the indictments of Amaya for three counts of tampering with governmental records and one count of engaging in organized criminal activity. A jury later found Amaya not guilty. Upon investigation by TCEQ, close to thirty violations were found at the plant, along with the discovery of E. coli in drinking water and none of the operators holding proper licenses. The Texas Rangers also found Amaya had asked employees to sell tickets for fundraisers and located lists from the water department's storage room of employees who owed money from ticket sales.

Amaya lost his re-election bid for the board of trustees for LISD in November 2014.

Another water boil notice boiled residents, but this time in Laredo when in September of 2019 the city issued a water boil notice alert for certain portions of the city and hours later rescinded their notice to apply it to the entire city, then the following morning call off the city-wide water boil notice and apply it only to certain portions of the city. The confusion is not the controversy, but rather the cause of the effect of the water boil notice.

Days after the alert, the city revealed that an anonymous source, a resident in El Azteca neighborhood reported on the condition of the tap water. The resident, Federico Reyes came forward of his identity and said he contacted the city weeks prior, but with no success, and that is when he contacted TCEQ. The findings of TCEQ through the source's contact made them aware of low-chlorine levels of the water causing the water boil notice alert. The Utilities Director Riazul Mia said there was "miscommunication" when the city announced the water boil notice, which caused thousands of residents to flood local stores and buy water causing temporary shortages of water supply in all local stores. Mia blamed the low-choline levels on stagnant water and high temperatures of summer.

Mia also told council in a special called meeting that Reyes had an external filtration system at his residence making the water test results skewed. Within days, the city went into a 30-day free chlorine burn making the tap water staunch of chlorine high. Mayor Pete Saenz told the media the water was "completely safe" and "very good water," however skeptical residents said the strong smell of chlorine chemicals caused concern and even environmental activist Erin Brockovich publicly said "Don't you believe it" regarding the water being safe. Brockovich said "the dangerous conditions are only going to get worse... the city is conducting a 30-day free chlorine burn to clear the water lines of any possible nitrates or lingering scum that could be responsible for bringing down disinfectant levels... get ready for toxic levels of chlorine byproducts and other potentially dangerous conditions!"

The city council voted to hire an independent investigative firm to look into the matter. The *Laredo Morning Times* revealed days later that the TCEQ had previously fined the city in 2016 for low-chlorine water levels in parts of north Laredo and Mia was quoted saying TCEQ should have fined the city in this instance instead of issuing a water boil notice as it is "a very scary notice."

Solicitation of a minor

Former Webb County Clerk Henry Flores was sentenced to eight years in prison on November 19, 2009, for solicitation of a minor. He pleaded guilty and allegedly saw an 11-year-old runaway boy wondering while driving and took him to Mall Del Norte.

He allegedly bought the boy underwear and took him to a movie theater. The boy alleged Flores propositioned him for sex and displayed pornographic material to the child. The prosecution dropped a second charge of displaying harmful material to a minor in return for a guilty plea.

Flores told the media that he picked up the boy on a boulevard and took him home to check his messages. Flores said he gave him a cigarette as the boy asked for one and lit one for him. He also said the boy walked into his bedroom and saw an opened pornographic magazine on his bed. Flores said the boy asked him if he had magazines with women in them and Flores said he did and showed him one. Flores then sat the boy on his lap and advised him to get his life straight and go back home. "It was always my intention to take the boy back to his own home. I didn't know what I was going to do because the boy was on some medication. Upon leaving a restaurant, I hugged the boy from behind and gave him a peck on his neck. He asked me if I was gay. I said no. I just told him that I was glad to have known him." Flores apologized to the boy's parents and the grief experiences during the boy's absence.

Flores left as Webb County clerk in December of 2002

Commissioner's bribes

David R. Cortez

Former Webb County commissioner David R. Cortez resigned from his position on January 25, 2005. Cortez was convicted in a bribery scandal as he admitted to funneling money to secure a prison contract. He pleaded guilty in 2005 for funneling near $39,000 in bribes to Willacy County commissioners in return for their votes to hire a consultant in a multi-million-dollar federal prison project.

He reached a plea bargain to cooperate with prosecutors in a federal and state investigation. A federal judge sentenced him to three months in prison and two years of supervised release with six months of home confinement. A $25,000 fine was also sentenced.

County Judge Louis H. Bruni appointed Cortez's daughter, Cindy Cortez Brunner the same day he resigned to replace him as a county commissioner. She lost to Attorney Sergio "Keko" Martinez where he received 57% of the vote in the 2006 election. In December of 2016, Cortez passed away.

Mike Montemayor

The case of former county Commissioner Mike Montemayor; this is one of the most highlighted corruption cases Webb County and Laredo has seen in most recent time. The FBI arrested former Precinct 1 Webb County Commissioner Kristopher Michael Montemayor in March of 2014, only a year and three months after taking office. He was sentenced on January 26, 2015, to serve 76 months in federal prison and pay a $109,405 fine for taking bribes.

Court records at the time stated Montemayor facilitated bribes with two other county commissioners and a city councilman but were not identified and were referred to as "uncharged co-conspirators." The alleged names of the individuals involved never came forth to the public or a court of law.

Montemayor asked and took cash and goods in exchange for obtaining people employment and business contracts. He accepted a 2012 Ford truck valued at $37,000 and in exchange offered government jobs to the truck's owner and his spouse. The former commissioner also accepted approximately $11,000 in cash and $2,700 worth of electronics from a local businessman. In exchange for these bribes, Montemayor offered to take official action in his elected capacity and promote the businessman's interests; the man happened to be an undercover law enforcement agent.

A timeline of the Montemayor bribery is as follows: on August 11, 2012, he was declared the winner in a recount vote by only ten votes. On September 12, a month later he accepted a white 2012 Ford F-150 truck. He was sworn into office on January 1, 2013, as Webb County Commissioner Precinct 1. From July 2014 through December 2013, Montemayor accepted $11,000 in cash and $2,700 in electronics. On July 11, 2013, he accepted $1,000 from an undercover agent and $5,000 in cash on August 8. He also accepted $5,000 from another undercover agent on October 23, 2013.

On December 7, 2013, Montemayor traveled to San Antonio, Texas staying at the Marriott River Center and attended a Spurs basketball game at the AT&T Center. The commissioner was met by FBI agents and questioned and admitted to working with three other elected officials.

On December of that month, he informed other people of him being approached by the FBI and made four recordings for the FBI, which did not prove useful to the agents.

He refused to cooperate further with the FBI unless Montemayor was given full immunity and the plea offer by government expired.

On February 27, 2014, Montemayor and his attorney met the FBI agents and refused to cooperate and return the electronic devises.

He was indicted by a grand jury for two counts of bribery on March 18, 2014 and was arrested and released on bond the following day.

On June 19, 2014, Montemayor pleaded guilty to one count of federal programs bribery

Case 5:14-cr-00252 Document 67 Filed in TXSD on 01/20/15 Page 14 of 25

In addition to the more than $120,000 Montemayor received or solicited for his personal benefit, the Court should consider the other benefits sought, and received, by Montemayor's uncharged coconspirators in calculating the loss amount. The broad language of U.S.S.G. § 2C1.1(b)(2), which states that the loss amount can be calculated to include "the value of anything obtained or to be obtained by a public official or others acting with a public official," encompasses the things of value obtained by uncharged individuals who conspired with Montemayor to commit bribery.[4]

Montemayor admitted that, prior to learning of this criminal investigation, he arranged meetings between the undercover FBI agent and other public officials for the purpose of facilitating bribe payments to those officials. Indeed, Montemayor admitted to conspiring with an elected member of the City Council to facilitate a $4,900 cash bribe payment provided by the undercover agent to the City Council member in exchange for the City Council member's favorable vote. FD-302, Dec. 7, 2013 interview, at 4. He also admitted to conspiring with a fellow County Commissioner to facilitate a $1,000 cash bribe payment provided by the undercover agent to the County Commissioner in exchange for her favorable vote on the Commissioners Court. Id. Montemayor also admitted he introduced the undercover agent to

and was sentenced to six years and four months in prison on January 26, 2015.

For Montemayor, this was not the first instance in which he was in trouble with the law. In 2001, Laredo police arrested Montemayor and charged him with public indecent exposure, where no charges were filed. In 2008, he was charged by the Webb County District attorney's office with theft; the D.A. later dropped the charge.

Montemayor speaks on corruption

Montemayor was interviewed by a social media radio show Gloves Off with Paul Buitron after being released from prison, admitting he committed the crime, saying "I'm not gonna lie, I did it, I pleaded guilty to a crime that I did commit."

Saying it is difficult to be an elected official as they have many people to please, and "when you don't vote the way others want you to vote, it comes back, it haunts you. You are never going to be right; you are never going to be wrong." Montemayor acknowledged he became tangled up in the corruption and is now focusing on stopping corruption because he was a corrupt official.

He said there are "different forms of corruption, which can be anything" from having a ticket taken off for helping a campaign or money being exchanged. Reiterating that it could be a "wink wink deal or bribes disguised as donations."

When asked if there is still corruption, Montemayor says, "corruption is huge" and there are many elected officials who talk about stopping corruption, "when they are corrupted themselves." He also says an elected official can "slip up without knowing" they did.

Regarding the April 2017 FBI raids, Montemayor says he believes there will be others prosecuted. He says once interviewed by the FBI, "you're going to jail" and calls it "scary".

He also tells elected officials to "slow down" if not they will lose it all.

Raffle money

On October 11, 2007, the Texas Attorney General's office executed a search warrant at the office of Webb County Tax Assessor-Collector Patricia Barrera. The agents took computers, files, and other forms relating to the office and lasted over four hours. Agents were searching for documents pertaining to Barrera's campaign finance records from October 2004 to October 2007.

Agents took documents related to possible use of receipts of raffle and football pot money. Barrera and other employees allegedly participated in football pots and raffles in which money collected was used to fund Barrera's campaigns. Documents stated Barrera allegedly violated the Texas Election Code prohibiting a candidate to unlawfully make or accept contributions and accept cash contributions more than $100 during a reporting cycle. She also allegedly violated Chapter 39.02 of the Texas Penal Code in abuse of official capacity.

Fired workers from her office filed a complaint in federal court resulting in the investigation. They stated Barrera fired nine employees from her office for refusing to gamble on football and mandatory raffles to raise funds for her campaigns. Plaintiffs stated since 1996, employees had to participate in four raffles a year and was mandatory for the employees. Barrera and three co-defendants under her "enforced participation in the raffles by verbal threats, intimidation and open hostility, including, but not limited to, the threat of termination, the threat that terminated employees would be black-balled from other government and non-government jobs, or other unspecified retaliation," the complaint stated.

Allegedly, 30 tellers in her office were issued at least twenty raffle tickets and ordered to sell them for a dollar to five dollars each.

Barrera publicly stated to the local news the allegations were nothing more than efforts to derail her campaign for re-election in 2008 and stated, "I have nothing to hide. I have nothing to be ashamed of."

In 2010, the two misdemeanor counts of possession of gambling paraphernalia were dismissed. The charges were dismissed after adhering to conditions set forth by a pretrial diversion program. Barrera was monitored for a year and had to pay a fee. She also had to forfeit almost $13,000 from the money raised by the raffles and ticket sales. A civil lawsuit against Barrera was also settled by the county footing a $950,000 bill to settle this lawsuit. Her attorney Donato Ramos stated, "We're glad it's over. We were always in the position that we were going to fight this; it was a victimless crime; she had nothing to hide." And while Barrera did not ultimately face any criminal prosecution, her chief deputy was indicted in 2008 as part of the state investigation into gambling

Barrera was re-elected in 2008 where she faced an opponent in the Democratic primary and 2012, she captured 83.6 percent of the vote with only a green party candidate opposition. She also ran for Webb County judge in 2018 after resigning her position as Tax Assessor-Collector, retiring from the county.

Police chief bribe

In October 2007, Laredo Police Department Police Chief Agustin Dovalina III pleaded guilty in a federal court for taking bribes and extortion in return for shielding illegal gambling operations in the city.

He admitted to taking in $13,500 in cash and golf equipment from various operators of 8-liner operations, known to many as "*maquinitas*." He retired immediately after that as police chief.

Dovalina and two of his subordinates, Sgt. Alfonso Santos and Police Lt. Eloy Rodriguez, who is a brother to Webb County Constable Rodolfo "Rudy" Rodriguez, also agreed to plead guilty and cooperate with the Federal Bureau of Investigations.

Dovalina told the press, "Today is one of the darkest, saddest days of my life… I want to apologize to my family, to my law-enforcement colleagues and especially to my community for having let them down."

According to Carlos Villarreal, the city manager at the time stated the plea from Dovalina would not affect the retirement benefits he has. Dovalina's attorney stated he was under great stress because of a financial crisis he was going through at the time. He blamed a heart attack and a house fire, thus lacking the judgment at the time.

Sexual harassment

Two former employees of Webb County Commissioner Frank Sciaraffa allegedly stated they were forced to perform sexual acts on him in 2012 and 2013 in a federal court suit.

A La Presa Community Center employee and a community center director made claims Sciaraffa forced the women to perform sex acts on him in order keep their jobs.

The former community service director claimed the commissioner forced her to give him a sexual act on a weekly basis and her duties would be dropped if a sexual harassment claim was filed. She started as a campaign assistant in the commissioner's 2004 campaign.

According to reports, Commissioner Sciaraffa promised the director to protect her and would have a job as long she takes care of it by performing the sexual acts. Documents claim some of the acts occurred in his office where the director was forced to perform oral sex on the commissioner.

The director alleged she had to stay in her job and was afraid of losing her job if she stopped committing the acts forced by the commissioner, as the job was her only source of income and needed health insurance.

In 2014 a judge dropped one claim of sexual harassment against the commissioner because for lack of evidence. The legal representation for the Webb County commissioner cost taxpayers over $80,000.

Sciaraffa however, admitted to some of the sexual contacts and stated it was consensual between him and the community director.

Sciaraffa lost re-election in his 2012 race where Mike Montemayor won by only ten votes. In 2014, Montemayor was forced to quit his seat after a bribery charge, and Sciaraffa was selected by the Webb County Democratic Party to run for his former seat in a November 2014 special election where he won against a Green Party candidate. Sciaraffa was unseated in 2016. He entered a Laredo College board of trustee race in November of 2016 and lost in a run-off election. He ran again for the trustee position at LC in 2018 losing to Lupita Zepeda.

In 2017, a settlement of a $200,000 payout was reached between Sciaraffa and the county employee. The settlement was paid from the county's private insurance coverage and not taxpayer money or public funds.

Justice of the Peace bribery

Former Webb County Justice of the Peace Ricardo Rangel pleaded guilty to extortion in September of 2014. Rangel admitted to accepting a bride while under official capacity as a judge in March of 2012. He accepted $250 from a bail bondsman in return for granting a $1,000 surety bail bond on a person who had been arrested and charged with driving while intoxicated.

Rangel resigned from his position, and a justice of the peace was appointed by the commissioner's court. He was sentenced to 37 months in prison on August of 2015.

At the time of the sentencing hearing in August of 2015 by U.S. District Judge Diana Saldana, authorities recorded Rangel taking about a dozen bribes throughout 2012. The crimes in which he reduced bonds for in exchange for bribes included criminal defendant's charges with aggravated assault, robbery, and kidnapping. Further discovery involved an instance where Rangel accepted a trip to Las Vegas for him and his wife paid for by a bail bondsman costing $1,700.

Judge Saldana stated Rangel was at a point where there was "no regard whatsoever with what the individuals were charged with."

Rangel attorney stated, "There is no excuse for what he did, and he wanted to make it crystal clear that he was accepting responsibility from the beginning."

The former justice of the peace told the media, "I know that I did wrong, but I did more good than wrong."

Previously on February 15, 2007, the DPS state troopers stopped him for driving while intoxicated and arrested Rangel. He was arrested for a similar offense in November of 1999, but the case was dropped.

He was first elected in 2002, was re-elected in 2006, 2010, and in 2014 by the voters.

Rangel was involved in a three-vehicle accident in the summer of 2017 where he was critically injured. Rangel survived the crash, but sustained life altering injuries. Rangel said he was grateful to be alive and in good spirits.

Taking signs

On October 13, 2014, Councilmen Alejandro "Alex" Perez, Jr. was arrested along with two of his campaign volunteers for allegedly stealing a political sign from one of his opponents, Abraham "Abey" Lugo, a DPS trooper. Perez was issued a citation for theft under $50.00, a Class C misdemeanor on the night of October 13.

On October 15th, Lugo released a cell phone video he taped while confronting Perez in a white Honda Pilot. The video shows the councilman telling Lugo "'*asi lo quieres jugar o que* bro", with Lugo telling Perez, "sir, I wouldn't be making threats like that." Perez told him "why don't you just take it and we'll call it even man, I mean, *ya* I won't mess around with your signs anymore, you just messing with my signs man, and we'll keep it clean."

The video showed by local media further shows Lugo asking Perez "Mr. Perez, can you tell me whose sign this is? "Perez responded, "yea, that's your sign." Lugo also asked him how it got in his vehicle, Perez responded, "they have been taking my signs, bro, I don't know if it's your people." He further went on to say, "I'm doing what you're doing to my signs bro." Lugo refuted this and stated he never done anything with Perez's signs.

The councilman told the media he was taking responsibility for the actions of the campaign worker and understood the property owner only wanted his signs to be placed on the property in question and not his opponent's sign. The councilman had told a group of Occupy Laredo in a 2011 city council meeting that he respected freedom of speech.

Perez pleaded not guilty in municipal court. Perez won re-election in a run-off against Lugo. The third candidate supported Perez in the run-off. In 2018, Perez ran unsuccessfully for Webb County Commissioner in precinct two challenging the incumbent "Wawi" Tijerina. Lugo ran against Perez's wife for city council in November of 2018 where a third candidate, Mercurio "Merc" Martinez III ultimately won in a run-off in which was endorsed by Lugo.

Rio Bravo Mayor

In May of 2014, Rio Bravo, Texas Mayor Manuel Vela, Jr. turned himself into the Webb County sheriff's department because of a pending warrant for numerous charges including engaging in an organized criminal activity, money laundering, and promotion of gambling.

He posted a $19,000 bond the evening of his arrest. Vela told the media, "As Mayor of the City of Rio Bravo, I want to assure to the community that my commitment to keep the citizens protected continues to be my priority."

Rio Bravo residents again saw more controversy from their mayor, this time in January of 2018 from Mayor Francisco Peña, a local physician. Dr. Peña was indicated for being connected to a health care fraud and money-laundering scheme worth $150 million. He was also charged with one count of false statements and one count of obstruction of a health care investigation. The indictment from the U.S. Attorney's Office alleged Peña along with physicians from a health care group caused kickbacks and bribes to be paid to them in return for certifying patients qualified for services when they did not qualify.

At a January city commission meeting, Peña presided over the meeting and no action was taken to remove him from his seat.

The town of Rio Bravo has continued its political controversy even after Dr. Peña retired from office. In the summer of 2019, residents launched a petition to recall their Mayor, Daisy Lee Valdez. Residents accused Valdez of taking $5,000 from the city's account to purchase gift cards. Valdez denied the accusations and said the money was used to fix a road that gives access to school buses for children to ride. The gift cards were purchased as a Walmart money card to pay in fixing the streets according to Valdez. Residents voted on the recall referendum election in the November 2019 elections.

County Attorney's office

In October of 2004, two Webb County attorney investigators under County Attorney Homero Ramirez were accused of paying thousands of dollars in payoffs in bribes for information on possible eight-liner "maquinetas" businesses.

The two employees of the county attorney's office and one owner of an eight-liner business were arrested on ten felony charges of bribery and one charge of engaging in organized criminal activity.

The eight-liner business were under constant surveillance, and the owner of this business allegedly worked hand-in-hand with these investigators to give them a heads up when a raid was to occur in the establishment.

County Court at Law II

Jesus "Chuy" Garza was indicted in January of 2017 on a misdemeanor influence peddling charge for a count of a gift to a public servant by a person in his jurisdiction, a Class A misdemeanor. Garza turned himself in after a warrant was issued and out on a $2,500 bond. He resigned following the indictment and pleaded not guilty in February. The Texas Attorney General's office prosecuted the case.

According to the indictment, In January of 2015, Garza solicited a $3,000 loan from Shirley Mathis for one of his employees, Christopher Casarez, a court coordinator. Garza allegedly asked Mathis for the loan in return to appoint her to civil dispute case on an estate for Carlos Y. Benavides, Jr. Garza was the presiding judge in the lawsuit involving Benavides' estate, in which Mathis was the guardian. In December of 2016, Casarez committed suicide at his residence before having to meet with authorities on the investigation.

Garza's brother, Laredo ISD board of trustee, Ricardo Garza told the media his brother's "charges are frivolous."

Later that month, allegations surfaced of Garza receiving kickbacks from attorneys and offering minimal sentencing in exchange for money. A complaint document filed by the State Commission on Judicial Conduct stated Garza awarded $20,000 to an attorney more than requested or entitled to receive, in return to have the attorney contribute those funds to his political campaign or the judge. The complaints were dismissed as Garza agreed to voluntarily resign from his position.

On March 27, 2017 after Commissioner John Galo had set a motion forth where the Webb County Commissioners Court voted to appoint Victor Villarreal for the Court at Law II seat. This came in with minor controversy as State Senator Judith Zaffirini's husband Carlos Zaffirini, an attorney, received an email from Villarreal stating his reasons for being the best candidate for the position and whether the Zaffirini's had any sway in the Commissioner's Court. Senator Zaffirini has publicly said earlier the court under Garza was the "absolute worst in the state" saying his court was the "textbook on cronyism."

A former employee of Garza's office was asked if these instances were known while employed. The person replied that there were many more things than we know going on at his office, but never said anything for fear of losing the job and would not elaborate further for fear of repercussions.

Judge Garza had served on the court since 1993 and had been re-elected since. On November of 2017, misdemeanor charges against Garza were dismissed in exchange for voluntarily resigning from the Texas Bar Association.

The FBI Raid

On the morning of Wednesday, April 26, 2017, the FBI raided City Hall along with the City Hall annex and the Public Works Department. The federal agents also stormed into the Webb County Courthouse, specifically the Webb County Engineering offices and the Webb County Precinct 4 Office under Commissioner Jaime Canales.

As word spread of the FBI being in Laredo, many were wondering on the reason for them being here. Later that day, people learned the FBI also raided several offices throughout the state of Dannenbaum Engineering, including their office in Laredo.

The mayor, county judge, including several city council members and county commissioners conducted a press conference regarding the raid but did not disclose any new details as the FBI had not released any information. City Hall and other city departments closed down as the investigation was being conducted.

The FBI searched for several documents from the city and county, including campaign reports and documentation relating to action taken between officials and Dannenbaum from January 1, 2013, to present. The public later learned the agents were searching for documents pertaining to public corruption. Several violations were being investigated, including mail fraud, wire fraud, theft or bribery, honest services, and the Hobbs Act, which according to the United States Department of Justice, prohibits actual or attempted robbery or extortion affecting interstate or foreign commerce "in any way or degree." Section 1951 also proscribes conspiracy to commit robbery or extortion without reference to the conspiracy statute at 18 U.S.C. § 371, which is a conspiracy to defraud the United States.

Specifically, the documents searched were for any dealings between the city, county, and the engineering firm, Dannenbaum. The search warrant included a list of target-subjects and a secondary list of other subjects of public officials.

Those on the target list include half of the city council, excluding the mayor. Mayor Saenz said the FBI told him, "It's not you" when the raid occurred at City Hall. Those on the target list include councilmembers Rudy Gonzalez, Jr, Alberto Torres, Roberto Balli, and Alejandro "Alex" Perez. Former Councilman Johnny Amaya, Juan Narvaez, and Roque Vela, Jr. were also listed as target subjects. State Representative Richard Raymond, City Manager Jesus Olivares and Louis Jones of Dannenbaum Engineering were also listed.

A secondary list includes city council members, Nelly Vielma, Charlie San Miguel, Vidal Rodriguez, and George Altgelt. Assistant City Manager Robert Eads was also listed along with the Traffic Safety Director, City Engineer, Utilities Director, and the Building Department Director. City Manager Jesus Olivares told the media, "We don't have anything to hide, and we'll provide everything that we're asked for." Several former and current elected officials came out on the media and social media expressing their intent to cooperate with the federal agents. Juan Narvaez said, "As elected officials, we took action on some of those contracts...sometime in the future they'll ask me about my vote." Representative Richard Raymond issued a statement saying he will assist the FBI with any request. Councilman Alberto Torres stated he had only been in office for several months and the investigation is "very broad, and we don't have any specifics..." and further said he would continue to do the job and be "business as usual." Councilman Alex Perez stated the investigation was ongoing and any further comments would be inappropriate at the time.

Mayor Pete Saenz called the raid "embarrassing" but welcoming. Commissioner John Galo told the media outside the courthouse, "Corruption in Webb County has been going for too long." In a press conference, County Judge Tano Tijerina said, "we, together, are going to be for justice, transparency and truth." Tijerina also said Dannenbaum has been one of Webb County's consultants on "anything having to do with Loop 20."

Records indicated Dannenbaum has several contracts with the city and county, including a $100,000,000 project for the city's El Pico Water Treatment Plant and over a million dollars in a contract awarded to Dannenbaum for a water line connection. The city council selected Dannenbaum without posting a request for proposals in December of 2014. City Manager Jesus Olivares stated this project would connect Mines Road to I-35 and open up over 6,000 acres of land for development. Webb County commissioner's court also approved a $2.4 million dollar contract for a Loop 20 project in August of 2013. State Representative Richard Raymond authored a House bill in 2015 to make the Hachar Loop project possible by allowing the city to designate four corridors for trucks with overweight and oversize cargo. The Hachar Loop is a proposed five-lane rural highway from Mines Road to I-35. On March 20th of 2017, city council approved an advanced funding agreement for this construction. A representative from Dannenbaum spoke in support of the advanced funding agreement before the council on March 20th, telling the council "you're pretty much getting that project for six cents on the dollar to the city and to the Laredo taxpayers. It's a good business model."

Several days after the raid, Dannenbaum's attorneys stated the raids of their offices all across Texas were a publicity stunt and accused federal employees of giving sensitive information on the investigation. The FBI denied these allegations. The FBI investigated James Dannenbaum, the CEO of the engineering firm in 2007 for allegedly masking bribes as political contributions to several El Paso officials. He was never charged with any wrongdoing; however, an El Paso County judge pleaded guilty to commit mail fraud and deprivation of honest services and was sentenced to federal prison in the corruption case. The judge accepted bribes and contributions in exchange for a favorable vote and influence on contracts.

On May 1, 2017, the Laredo City Council voted to hire an outside attorney to counsel the city in avoiding a similar incident as the FBI raid. Mayor Saenz proposed this idea with the council voting for it except Councilmen Vidal Rodriguez, who stated the city did not need "extra counsel to tell us what's right or wrong" saying it's in the individual's conscience.

The council also voted to put any pending business with Dannenbaum Engineering on hold on May 8th of that year. The city had three projects with Dannenbaum at the time along with a pending light synchronization project. Councilmen Roberto Balli, Alex Perez, and Vidal Rodriguez voted against this item. Atlgelt said, "There is a cloud. We should err on the side of caution," while Balli argued the city could risk losing federal funding or have potential lawsuits if the projects would be placed on hold.

As two years had passed after the FBI raid, the public became wary nothing was to come of it. However, on the morning of October 17, 2018 County Commissioner Jaime Canales unexpectedly resigned from his position and hours later, the U.S. Attorney's Office announced a guilty plea from Canales for conspiracy to commit bribery. Canales pleaded guilty along with former Councilman and LISD Trustee, Johnny Amaya.

The charges stemmed from the April 2017 FBI raid of City Hall and the County Courthouse. Both Canales and Amaya were target subjects on the FBI's search warrant list and Canales' office was the only one searched by the FBI. The U.S. Attorney's office indicated Canales accepted checks disguised as campaign contributions in addition to entertainment and meals totaling over $5,000. The checks were made from an individual attempting to influence and reward the commissioner for favorable actions on commissioner's court and as a representative on a TxDot committee. At an October 17, 2016 Metropolitan Planning Organization meeting Canales voted to approve a plan that secured funds for a $4.6 million contract modification benefiting Dannenbaum Engineering. On the other hand, Amaya owned JAUC Service Inc. and employed by a co-conspirator, later identified as Louis H. Jones Jr. principal/director for Dannenbaum Engineering's South Texas region as a consultant for "Corporation A" or Dannenbaum Engineering where he contacted various county and city officials directing them to take actions benefiting the co-conspirator and corporation. Furthermore, Amaya kept close contact with the officials in assisting the conspirator and corporation set up meetings and relaying messages to and from the conspirator. The former councilman and trustee acted as a middleman between the conspirator and public officials. The release further stated Amaya supported "specific candidates in the November 2016 election cycle by providing rental cars, drivers and gas cards for those rental vehicles to transport voters to the polls, all for which the corporation paid." The release did not name the candidates involved in the November 2016 election.

Days later on October 22, 2018 Dannenbaum engineer Louis H. Jones was found dead by suicide to what his family said died at a "place he chose" and not at his home in McAllen.

Dannenbaum Contributions

Campaign finance reports show numerous local city, county, state, and federal officials receiving political contributions from Dannenbaum. All four incumbent Webb County Commissioners along with the county judge received contributions from Dannenbaum. John Galo received $15,000, Jaime Canales $10,500, Wawi Tijerina $5,000 and Commissioner Jesse Gonzalez received $3,350. County Judge Tano Tijerina received $5,000.

Former Commissioner Frank Sciaraffa also received $17,500 in total from James Dannenbaum and wife, and Louis James from 2007 through 2011. On the city council, seven out of the eight council members received contributions from Dannenbaum. Councilman Vidal Rodriguez, Roberto Balli, and Rudy Gonzalez all received $2,000 each. Councilmen George Altgelt and Alberto Torres each received $2,500. Councilman Charlie San Miguel received $500.

Former Councilman Roque Vela, Esteban Rangel, and Juan Narvaez also received donations from Dannenbaum during their time in office. An unnamed local engineer told *Laredo Morning Times* that Louis H. Jones, director of Dannenbaum Engineering in South Texas had a close relationship with council members, commissioners, and other elected officials by giving them various types of support, such as contributing to campaigns and buying tables at events. John Galo told the media he had a professional relationship with Louis Jones, stating the real issue here is with the people who do not report the donations when asked about his $15,000 contribution from Jones. County Judge Tijerina said he and Jones have had a "cordial relationship, nothing personal."

According to campaign reports from 2000 through 2017, State Representative Richard Raymond had accepted $46,000 in total from Louis Jones and James Dannebaum. State Senator Judith Zaffirini also received $6,000 from Louis Jones and another $48,500 from James and Shirley Dannenbaum for a total of $54,500 in contributions. Finally, United States Congressman Henry Cuellar accepted a total of $42,900 in contributions from Jones and the Dannenbaum's, being the ninth-highest paid elected official in the federal government in 2015-2016.

Zaffirini issued a statement stating she has known James Dannenbaum since 1993 and said Dannenbaum "has contributed to many statewide, congressional, and legislative candidates, and I always appreciate his generosity..." She further mentioned he has not been charged and innocent until proven guilty.

Chapter 9:

CAÑONEROS

Former Mayor JC Martin once said it was possible to deliver eight to ten thousand votes to a specific candidate chosen by the *patrón* by analyzing the situation and seeing who would best serve South Texas or a certain district in Laredo to decide whom to deliver the votes to. The eight to ten thousand votes could not only influence local elections, but also statewide races where Martin says is how they were able to make themselves heard in the "legislature, in the state senate, and into national politics."

When asked by reporter Bill Moyers if there were tricks to help poor people vote, Martin said, "…there used to be all types of tricks to teach people how to vote, there used to be the marked ballot."

The marked ballot is still used in some form in today's election by the *cañoneros* to teach people how to vote or who to vote for.

In Laredo, the honest truth in most if not all elections involve the use of *cañoneros* or *politiqueras*, otherwise known as vote-getters. This is not just being a community organizer and engaging people in a democracy to participate in elections and exercise their vote. This is more complex than that, of course.

Since the days of Mayor Martin's *patrón* politics, the type of delivering votes to certain candidates never changed, however, the number of groups delivering votes to certain candidates has. In some way, the *patrón* style of delivering the vote evolved.

We are infiltrated with professional voter getters who take voters out to the polls in droves and tell them who to vote for. These *cañoneros* target the elderly from relatives to those in nursing homes. They also pinpoint the much less educated voters and those who do not speak English too well. Many instances these are the voters who are intimidated and are told who to vote for.

These vote-getters are contacted by a candidate, groups of candidates, or certain politicians and are made aware of which candidate to get the vote out for. These individuals usually contact residents from the precincts or locations the candidate or multiple candidates are running in and tell them they will be picked up to take them to the polls and are told who they need to vote for, of course. They usually have on hand a copy of a sample ballot and circle the candidate or candidates they need to vote for.

Some of the time, a candidate or a representative will ask a *cañonero* to create a list of voters they have taken or told to vote for them. This list includes the name of the voter and the date they voted so they can crosscheck with the elections office to confirm their vote. A list of voters during early voting is compiled daily by the elections office and provided to a candidate running for office upon request. The voter list includes full legal name, residence address, date of birth, and precinct number.

Most of the so-called bought or delivered votes occur during early voting. Numbers on some candidates from early voting totals piled up votes mostly from early voting, and then on Election Day, the tallies of votes received were much closer.

A *cañonero* is paid, otherwise, why would they be doing it for democracy? This is not a democracy! Typically, these vote getters are paid for each vote they can get for a candidate. The amount of money paid per vote depends, ranging from $10, $25, to $30 a vote. Some have reported being paid more than just cash, and in return receive jobs when a candidate is elected. Others are paid in gas cards or gift cards.

In some instances, the vote getter is never paid money but promised jobs for them or a relative. Buying votes are illegal and go unreported in campaign finance report expenses, offering a job to someone in return for votes is bribery, but unfortunately, it happens way too often.

You also have individuals who work as the political right-hand man for a living. In these cases, some candidates report the expense of a handyman on their campaign finance reports as "campaign workers," when in fact these individuals do more than just display their signs all over town in their vehicles or place political signs all around the city for them, or stand on sidewalks holding signs. You see, these individuals are in a way manipulated by the candidate with money, they are being paid legally, after all, these individuals mostly uneducated get people to vote as a *cañonero* and help with getting people to vote for the candidate who is paying them.

One of these individuals stated to a candidate not to run if they do not have the funds to pay for someone to get votes or place signs – that they should not run. Imagine that!

There are reports of local nursing homes, adult daycares and assisted living centers where these vote getters visit people from these places often buying their votes by taking them food such as sweet bread and barbecue and "help them" vote.

Cañoneros state these people want company and want someone to talk to and feel needed; this is when they become exploited for the political process.

As Webb County and Laredo is a democratic stronghold, many election contests are decided in the democratic primaries, which make the jobs of a *cañonero* crucial to ensure a victory. These *cañonero*s are powerful and steer the poor and uneducated to the right lawyer, social service agency, or officeholder to solve their problems. These vote getters, much like community organizers reach their community and help them in exchange for their voice to be voted on by someone else.

The *cañonero* is not only paid, or given jobs, but also wined and dined, invited to high-society events, and paid trips to state party conventions.

In truth, most if not all candidates rely on them as every candidate is approached. One of the candidates I spoke to feared being identified because there was a high possibly their votes from the *cañonero* would be sold to the opponent.

From personal experience of running a campaign, I know personally how the use of *cañoneros* affects democracy.

In my 2014 campaign, I was offered to get votes for a cost more than one instance and refused. Why? Because I did not have the grand funds of a highly funded campaign, firstly, secondly, it is unethical and illegal; thirdly, it defeats the purpose of democracy. On the other hand, some people approached me and supported my campaign with their votes without anything in return, but my trust that I would serve them to the best of my ability if elected.

In the end, it is better to lose wisely than to win corrupted and promised.

These vote getters are very reminiscent of the Old Party days when people voted for a candidate or "party" because their life depended on it.

In my 2016 campaign, I had to see and hear it to truly believe it to the ultimate truth. Thinking to myself, does this really happen? Do candidates really win on using *cañoneros*? Therefore, I did. I had to see and hear it with my own eyes and ears. It does happen in this Laredo democracy.

A gentleman I met with said he helped an opponent of mine in 2014 get elected by using *cañoneros* in a certain area of town. You see, there are several groups of individuals doing these services each election season all around town. It can become very expensive outside of any political expenditure report to use *cañoneros* in an at-large race, but it does happen and can be done. This same individual I met with said a candidate up for re-election in city council provided him with a vehicle and $1,000 in cash to help the candidate receive votes. The individual has a list of registered voters he takes to the polls and tells them how to vote. Most of the people on the list showed were the elderly or impoverished.

Another *cañonera* shortly arrived after that and told me she had her own list of voters, some deceased, which ballots, were already being mailed out. Saying, "This could not happen too much on the north side of town because, you know how it is over there, and they report everything to everyone." Yes, democracy involves many deceased voters choosing who will represent you. This happens when the Webb County elections office does not work hand-in-hand with other offices to look into those who are registered to vote but deceased. The deceased can vote because of this and because their relatives can request their ballots be mailed out (mail-in ballots), thus voting for their deceased relatives.

The individual also admitted many elected officials take "legal kick-backs" while in office and benefit from contracts given out in return for legal, political contributions when they are up for re-election. This way, the *cañonero* can be paid more next time they run, as they will have more money then. The individual said this was O.K. as long as they are careful not to do anything illegal and mess up doing so. They just want to "help and in turn benefit" from their community.

Any elected official who tells you they never used the type of vote gathering tactic is lying. The mafia of the *cañoneros* are like a game of competition to candidates running for office. As candidates are up to the highest bidder and the one who pays more, will get their votes delivered. Other groups of *cañoneros* vie to choose their candidate where money or promises may or may not be involved. Arguably, some *cañoneros* or community organizers for those groups or individuals who do not want to be called as such, do not charge and simply choose a candidate who best fits their political needs.

You may wonder if all candidates do this - the answer is no. We have honest candidates who run independently on their own right and issues, but I guarantee you that they never win. It pains me to admit it, but that is the unfortunate and inconvenient truth.

The *cañonero* is a business and very frequent during election seasons, this when these low-income individuals resort to be a *cañonero* to be able and bring food to the table for their loved ones. Candidates benefit if they can afford it, while those making profit do it because of need, and the one who loses is democracy.

Chapter 10:

POLITICAL GROUPS AND CONTROL

Laredo had the *"Guaraches"*, the *"Botas"*, and the *"Partido Viejo"* way before we had what are now just the conventional political parties. Today we may not have the *"patron"* party of JC "Pepe" Martin, but there are still groups wanting to control certain aspects of our city, county, and state governments.

In almost every election race in this community, we see many candidates and or elected officials aligned with one candidate or another to ensure their victory on Election Day. Today, much like "cliques" various candidates and elected officials align to ensure further power plaguing in our city, county, and even at our schools.

Saying there is a particular person like a JC Martin of today controlling these "groups" would be incorrect, but rather what we see today are several individuals holding power in elected and public offices wanting to take control of more seats. We can see this in races where candidates are included from a "relative of a relative" or someone usually associated with another candidate from another race or elected official, usually by their employment, friendship or political *"padrino"*.

For instance, you can have a justice of the peace running for re-election in any given year, and there are a county commissioner and constable race in the same area he or she represents and will throw their support or people (voters) to them to ensure their "people" are elected.

In elections, you have had candidates who ran against each other in the past, then supported one another after. This is how politics in Laredo makes for strange bedfellows.

We have seen this with Bruni, Sciaraffa, and Casso on how they each politically defriended each other. Even in the family is political defriending not immune; Justice of the Peace Ricardo Rangel encouraged his brother-in-law, Ramiro Veliz, Jr. to run for his opposite seat in 2006, they ran together and won. Eventually, they disbanded politically and had candidates run against one another in future elections. In the 2006 race for Texas State Representative, District Attorney Joe Rubio, a cousin of Richard Raymond endorsed Raymond's opponent, Mercurio Martinez, Jr.

Much like history repeating itself of when the *"botas"* and *"guaraches"* merged, some of our current officials align, then disband, then maybe align again.

In 2008, Webb County saw a sheriff's race starting with six men vying for the job to remove the incumbent, Flores. Rick Flores defeated former Sheriff Juan Garza in 2004, a 16-year incumbent with 55% of the vote.

Upon entering office, Flores fired eighty employees in which he stated wanted to get rid of "dead weight" and corruption in the department.

Therefore, in the 2008 race for sheriff and his re-election saw five candidates running against him. Challengers included Martin Cuellar; Esteban Paez, one who filed a lawsuit against Flores for being fired; Gerardo "Jerry" Carmona and Jose "Pepe" Salinas, both of whom worked for former Sheriff Garza; and Anselmo "Chemo" Ortiz, a Laredo police department lieutenant. Ultimately, Paez and Salinas wound up working for

Cuellar when he was elected, and Salinas was elected for Justice of the Peace in 2014. Cuellar supported Salinas in his race.

The political parties in the nation have their special interests where they lobby a government official to vote their way or vote to get a government contract or funding. Here is no different, but instead of a Washington lobbyist strong-arming an elected official, we have wealthy building contractors, business people, bankers, and such wanting to get their piece of the pie when a new building is to be built, or a local government entity is about to award a contract. Like the saying goes, "money talks, and..." well you know the rest, or as my grandfather used to say, "*con el dinero, el perro baila*" or with money, the dog can dance. One can just follow the money and votes to know why someone is supporting whom.

Chapter 11:

ARE THE VOTERS GUILTY OF CORRUPTION?

Some people may say they do not vote because, well "why vote?" it is all the same corrupt politics as usual and it will never change. Some vote, a vote sometimes without being educated on the issues of the candidates running. This is when the voters can become guilty of continuing the corruption.

You have read how many elected officials have been arrested on crimes, corruption charges, and committed political favors for their benefit but still manage to get re-elected or get into office. The only one's holding them back from not being re-elected or voted into office is well, the voters. It is the voter's choice on who they vote in the voting booth, as only you will know whom you voted for.

Our community since its dawn of the day of elections has seen very low voting numbers in all elections. In fact, Webb County has more registered voters than actual voters who go to the polls each election season.

There are positive and negative reasons why people do or do not vote. One can ask a person why they do not vote and say how elected officials are typical and never get any real progress done only during an election season when wanting a vote.

It is during election season when you see many incumbents, new candidates and candidates to be out and about in pubic festivities, parades, get-togethers, and in the media to receive exposure to receive a vote, a grandstanding personality indeed.

Other reasons people do not vote are because of the favoritism and corruption constantly seen on the news and are turned off to go and vote to believe they will be contributing to this. When in reality, a non-voter only contributes to the breed of more corruption. The *cañoneros* win when a clean vote is wasted.

On the other hand, there are other reasons heard through the grapevine from people of people, or a friend of a friend who know elected officials themselves and how they do favors for one another, how one got a job because of a certain elected official, or how one got "away with it" because they know so and so.

I get it - this is merely a "you scratch my back, I'll scratch yours" kind of deal. This is again how the old *patron* party politics were played back then, which has not ended now. I know, I get them - these are several reasons why they do not vote.

Furthermore, we also see how often the same people vote in each election cycle, thus electing the same politicians. Just look at all the races every election season, as usually there are candidates who were term-limited or an incumbent running for a different position to have a chance of furthering their elected official status. A former city-council member running for school board or commissioner, a relative of a current or past elected official running for their old position. Political recycling happens, be it good or bad it is what it is because the same people are always involved, those who do vote and participate. Just imagine if those who did not vote did participate. What would happen? What would happen when voters were informed of the issues from the candidates? Would our elected officials look different from now?

Often time you see a politician or candidate offering change, however, all that will truly change is the person in the seat. The reason to vote is simple: your vote does count, and the only way to change this system of corrupted politics is to dismantle the usual politics, as we know it with your vote.

Yes, we do have candidates and elected officials who want to be elected for the common good and work for the people, placed there because they truly want to serve. Just like a troop serving their country because they believe in it and give their heart out to serve, an elected official or candidate should choose to run and stay elected because they are serving the people and our country, our democracy. We, the voters, we the people are the bosses to elected officials, and it is the time to realize they are in there because we got them in there. They can be replaced as easily as they were elected.

One person can begin to make these politicians held accountable for their actions and not be afraid to challenge them. There is a call on those apathetic voters and political activists to unite and vote for real change. The minority, those who do not vote are the majority, so go at it - vote.

Those who vote because they are promised a job, those who vote because a candidate buys their vote, those who vote because they are uneducated on the candidate running, and those who vote because they will benefit in some form from a corrupt act of an elected official. You are guilty of corruption, but it does not have to be this way.

Chapter 12:

ISSUES IN LAREDO AND WHY VOTING MATTERS

There are many issues popping up every day and this one reason why a vote is important and even more important to understand the issues of each candidate when running for office.

Many people do not get involved in understanding the issues on hand or know what a candidate running for office has to offer if elected. The elected officials placed in various offices have so much influence in the future and each person's daily lives, from the amount of taxes paid to local ordinances and laws, and infrastructure - everyone can be the influence, to be involved, because this is about all of us, our future, our community of Laredo and Webb County.

One asks why vote? It does not matter, when whom one votes into office matters because of what happens in our daily lives whether we like it or not. The streets we drive on every day and the condition these streets are in are there and in this condition because of the people you place in office.

The quality of your water as what happened in El Cenizo and Rio Bravo, and in Laredo has a direct connection of whom you place into office. The officials you elected to office determine the amount of taxes one pays. Any fee permits requirements, and costs are set forth by your elected officials. Washington and Austin see the voter turnout in our area and determine how much funding and attention we get from these "big shots" up there, with the low voting numbers we do not have much political clout up there.

The issues matter

The City of Laredo adopted the plastic bag ban in which retailers in the city could not use plastic bags provided to consumers. Stores such as H-E-B would not provide customers with bags, and they have to bring their own reusable bags to place their groceries, other stores such as Wal-Mart provide paper brown bags to their customers in place of the banned plastic bags. This is an example of how government directly affects you – the voter. In 2018, the state Supreme Court ruled against the bag ban ordinance after a lawsuit from downtown merchants and allowed plastic bags to be reinstated in stores.

In 2015, the city also implemented a full ban on using any electronic device while driving. This happened after a driver allegedly used his phone and struck women with his vehicle in Jacaman Street and one woman died. Council voted to ban the use of cell phone while driving as a result, thus impacting drivers (voters) directly by not being able to use their cell phone while driving.

In 2011, the citizens of Laredo started seeing many beer runs popping out all over the city, especially in the south. Beer runs under the names of Mami Chulas, Papi Chulos, Zebras Drive Thru, and Express Lane Drive Thru were located in high traffic areas in parts of town where they would have dancers in front of the businesses dancing with minimal clothes on, some in a sexual nature. People claimed these businesses offered more than just an eye view and offered what some call, prostitution. Some were in front of churches and schools. Former councilman Esteban Rangel, who represented areas that included several of these establishments told the media it was getting out of hand and would see some girls "humping the floor" in public.

The city attorney stated state law did not have anything against these establishments and the attendees dancing outside the beer runs were not breaking any local or state laws. In 2015, two beer-run owners were arrested for employing a 15-year-old minor.

If sexual-esque establishments do not affect you or your family, the City of Laredo voted in September of 2012 to set fees for when a person sets up a garage sale at their home. A garage sale permit is now required in the city to obtain before conducting a garage sale. An applicant must pay $5.00 for two days and wait four months to obtain another permit. Some argue why the city would charge for such a thing. And claim the city is only finding ways to make money when a garage sale is not something one usually makes to be profitable and just want to get rid of their old shirts or furniture. Now one can be fined if a permit is not obtained by the city if conducting a garage sale.

In May of 2019, city council voted to increase the water and sewer rates by five percent over the next five years. Council members said the increases will help pay for 178 million dollars investing in new water and sewer infrastructure.

Not much time later, it was revealed that the city would sue civil engineers, constructors, inspectors, and managers who helped build El Pico Water Treatment Plant, which opened in 2015 for multiple water pump failures. Two of the three pumps malfunctioned and failed in the fall of 2016 costing the city $640,000. The third pump also failed in late spring of 2017. El Pico cost the city approximately $96 million and was designed by Dannenbaum Engineering, which also conducted construction oversight. The water treatment plant provides water for north Laredo.

In February of 2016, the FBI arrested all but one city council member, including the mayor for corruption in the small town of Crystal City, Texas just a few hundred miles north of Laredo. This was not only a problem because of the obvious, but also days later residents started seeing "black sludge" water pouring out of their faucets, thus creating more problems for this community. One, the residents could not trust any of their elected officials and second, they were not any officials around to deal with this problem.

This is a prime reason why it matters who someone votes for because think about it, what if this happened in Laredo? Whom you elect in office has a direct result on your community. The residents of Crystal City voted these corrupt officials in and now were faced with this dilemma. Water is a necessity of life and extends beyond any political office or candidate, but there is no doubt the people who we place in office effect issues we face every day and even with the water, we drink and use in our daily lives.

Whether you agree or not with any of the ordinances set in place by our local government, these laws affect you directly in your daily lives, this is why voting is important because it is how one can control what is in place or is not.

Sometimes the voters get to decide on referendums such as new schools for school districts or new facilities for the city and county or a new jail such as in late 2017 when voters overwhelmingly denied a proposition from the county to build a new jail facility and law enforcement center for the county. The Sheriff's Department touted this proposition highly but over 65% of the voters did not support it at the polls.

Turned off voters?

Understandably, one can argue how they simply are "turned off" to vote when election campaigns get nasty. Some say they simply do not have a choice of candidates running or they the other ones who will just be the same.

In the 2012 race for Webb County sheriff, a race between Martin Cuellar and Rick Flores was one of the most contentious races Webb County had seen.

Cuellar was quoted in the Texas Tribune in a 2012 article calling Flores an "idiot" and Flores stated the sheriff's office was plagued by corruption and had concerns on the morale of workers and civil service concerns. In this election year, Flores attempted to regain the seat, but the Webb County Democratic Party challenged his residency requirements at the time and was forced to run as an independent where he lost.

That same year the race for Webb County commissioner between Sciaraffa and Louis H. Bruni became heated when lawsuits were involved alleging Sciaraffa of non-payment of loans and interest totaling more than $59,000. Bruni and Sciaraffa were one-time political allies and ran against each other in several races after that. Serving in an elected capacity can sometimes leave one feeling horrified. In October of 2009, Webb County Commissioner Frank Sciaraffa found his residence with about nine bullet holes on the part of the house after a drive-by shooting. The incident occurred at twelve in the morning, and no injuries were reported, only damage to the house. Laredo Police did not state who might have caused this.

When a campaign is in full effect, at times there are instances of candidate's signs gone missing or vandalized. We saw this with the city council district three race between Alex Perez and Abbey Lugo.

In 2006, former Mayor Raul Salinas had found several of his signs in a dumpster belonging to a fast food restaurant. Constable Rudy Rodriguez found several of his signs stolen and had been set on fire allegedly by some of his opponent's crewmember. A candidate for Webb County commissioner in 2016, Jesse Gonzalez saw ten of his signs found in a dumpster, the candidate stated he received a call from a supporter who saw two men in a white Ford Mustang throwing his signs.

In 2016, city council district four candidate Allen Tijerina had several of his signs taken off, including some instances where his signs were covered by those of opponent's Alberto Torres' signs. Tijerina told the media, "I did not want to think that it was any of my opponents until we found Alberto Torres' sign overlapping mine in a property where he does not have permission to put up a sign." Torres denied any involvement and said this was "childish and irresponsible."

In my own campaign, signs would go missing or vandalized and at worse at times would be removed and replaced by an opponent's sign. Opponents would deny they were directly or indirectly responsible, of course.

In late 2015 the city council district two race saw two candidates, Vidal Rodriguez and Annette Ugalde-Bonugli, a daycare owner in court when Bonugli's juvenile record became public and leaked. She claimed Rodriguez was involved in the leak and sued him. Rodriguez was a court coordinator for Justice of the Peace, Danny Dominguez and resigned two days after Dominguez was re-elected in March of 2016. Bonugli did not make the run-off in the five-candidate race and saw Rodriguez and Jose Perez III, a high school principal in the run-off. The case continued into the run-off also involving an arrested warrant for Councilman Esteban Rangel who was in a heated race for county commissioner against Webb County sheriff's captain Jesse Gonzalez. Rangel's attorney said the claims against his client were politically motivated because the Webb County sheriff's office named Rangel in a criminal complaint alleging he intended to disclose Bonugli's information, later the arrest warrant was dropped by the district attorney's office. However, the sheriff's department arrested Rodriguez a week before the run-off election. Ultimately, Rodriguez narrowly defeated Perez in the run-off on April of 2016.

Once elected, after a plea of no contest in August of 2017, on October 11th Councilman Rodriguez was found guilty by Webb County Court at Law I Judge Hugo Martinez of disclosing the criminal history of a former opponent. He was sentenced to one-year probation receiving deferred adjudication for accessing the record of Bonugli. Mayor Saenz told the media Rodriguez should consider resigning, while Bonugli stated the residents of district two had made a mistake in voting for him, and now it was up to them to make it better. Less than a week later city council reached no official decision on the status of Rodriguez's right to hold his seat. In what was a contiguous two-hour long debate at city council chambers, council ultimately voted four to two stating the crime for which Rodriguez was convicted of did not constitute moral turpitude, thus effectively keeping Rodriguez as councilman.

Councilman Altgelt who voted against said this sets precedence on any future council member who may be convicted of such crime. Many of Rodriguez's supporters were in attendance at council chambers wearing yellow shirts and showing their support for the councilman. Opponents also spoke out against Rodriguez, including the district attorney's office and Bonugli. At the meeting, Rodriguez blasted the mayor for opposing him saying an ongoing lawsuit between the mayor and his brother alleging Saenz owed the brother over $7 million in a trust is also considered moral turpitude. Rodriguez won re-election in 2018.

Heated races and political controversy

LareDos, a now defunct independent alternative monthly print newspaper sued former Laredo Mayor Raul G. Salinas in federal court for accusing him of violating their first amendment rights by having ordered to remove a May/June 2007 issue of LareDos from City Hall and the Laredo International Airport.

A surveillance video of the airport showing Salinas ordering the removal of the newspapers was sent to the public and showed the mayor telling an airport employee to remove the newspapers from a stand in the convention and visitors' section of the airport.

Salinas made a public apology at a council meeting stating he removed the issues because he did not want visitors to have a bad impression of Laredo.

The newspaper included an article criticizing the mayor for the role in approving a lease or sale of the city airport property for the building of a mall on the land, which included the Casa Blanca wetland. The issue also included a cartoon using skeletons to portray the mayor and his dog, Princess. Maria Eugenia Guerra said the removal of the newspaper was retaliation and is unconstitutional.

The proposed mall on the wetland was met with public outcry and petitions demanding any development to take place. No development in the wetland occurred until in late 2016 development of a mall began on this very land.

In a 2016 municipal race, the city council district five race between incumbent Roque Vela, Jr. and attorney Nelly Vielma became heated. After the election, Vela stated in a radio program he had spent an "obscene and unheard of" amount of money to campaign for re-election but was still outspent two to one by his opponent, Vielma. He said, "there was a lot of money that wasn't reported" and "unofficially spent" on radio ads and mail outs that "did not pop up on the finance report", he stated, "where did they come from?" Final campaign reports showed Vela spent $76,628 and Vielma spending $54,457.

During the campaign, Vela reported to the media on October of 2016 that his personal email account had been hacked. His statement read his account was hacked around September and believed the breach was intentional and related to the current political campaign for re-election. His opponent, Vielma denied any involvement of the hack. Around the same time, the *Laredo Morning Times* and *El Mañana de Nuevo Laredo* released articles three weeks before the election stating two sitting councilmen up for re-election, Roberto Balli and Roque Vela, Jr. had been arrested when teens.

Reports from the media stated Vela was arrested in San Antonio for possessing twenty-two pounds of marijuana, a marijuana plant, plastic bags congaing marijuana and other drug paraphernalia, including syringes, a weighing scale with a handgun along with one magazine and a box of ammunition at the age of 19 in 1996. He was also arrested in 1999 for disorderly conduct in Abilene, Texas.

Vela released a statement saying, "It was a life-changing event that shaped the man I am today." He further stated, "It's not how your story starts, but how it finishes. That I believe is how people will remember one." Vela's opponent, Nelly Vielma denied any involvement with the arrest record being released and told the media she was running based on her opponent's voting record, not his arrest record. However, a political advertisement on television later showed a hint of Vela's arrest record showing Vela speaking at a previous forum. Vela said Cliffe Killam, a partner at Killam Oil Company and developer and others hired attorney's to "dig" into his past and said his history was not a secret and his opponent in the 2012 race for city council; Pat Campos "never went there."

Balli, on the other hand, was arrested in 1984 at the age of 17 for driving while intoxicated in Travis County. Balli later said the case was dismissed as he completed community service hours and taking a sobriety course.

The 2016 municipal election saw more controversy when on August 24, 2016, the Laredo city secretary's office disqualified three candidates for city council in districts four, seven and eight after stating these candidates did not meet certain required documents or had missing content to the application forms for a place on the ballot.

District seven Councilman George Altgelt, an incumbent who was one of the candidates disqualified stated some candidates were advised about errors on the application and allowed to be corrected, but other candidates such as himself were not. Altgelt stated, "The city secretary failed to perform a statutory function – to review an application, within five days of receipt, and provide written notice of any deficiencies."

After a lawsuit filed by Altgelt and a court hearing, the city and Altgelt came to an agreement and had all of the city council candidates' names on the ballot for their perspective candidacy of each district. City Manager Jesus Olivares told the media mistakes were made by the secretary's office and many of the staff had only been there for a few months. After the lawsuit had been settled, the city footed the bill for nearly $15,050 to Altgelt's attorney along with spending $5,000 for hiring outside attorneys for the case.

In January of 2017, an audio recording of a behind closed door casual conversation of Councilman Roque Vela, Rudy Gonzalez, Juan Narvaez, and Mayor Pete Saenz surfaced on social media. The recording involved a conversation among them about mudslinging at city hall and a drug follicle testing done by all council members excluding one of their fellow council members.

The recording starts with Vela saying to Saenz, "I'm not going to partake in mudslinging, council isn't for that." Saenz responds by saying, "When you state that statement saying it's unprofessional that I am not going to partake in the mudslinging, I think people will understand that". Gonzalez then questions Saenz, "have you seen the video mayor?" the mayor then says, "*nomas pedacitos*," they're going to have it, I was going to see it at this weekend…" Narvaez then interrupts saying "…but I tell you what really happened, and why we are having this conversation, and I say, you're in a platform to clear, you said…I want to clean City Hall…" Saenz then said, "*no pos* I don't if I may have… (laughing) maybe, but when we run we exaggerate *un poquito, pero tabueno*," I'm okay with that". Narvaez telling him "you said that," then telling Saenz, "*ahora yo de dije oye Perez* (Councilman Alex Perez) *vas a dejar que de agarre del pinche pelo… no lo a echo*". Saenz then told Narvaez, "and I ask him, *pero podemos forsar?*" Narvaez tells him "if you have the honor, the honor, *luego, luego*." Saenz goes on and says he does not have much control and Narvaez telling him, "you're the mayor."

In March of 2018, the Texas Attorney General's office sent a letter to the county that it was investigating the county's 2018 March 6th primary election for mail-in ballot fraud. Jose S. Tellez, the interim Elections Administrator at the time said his office was not involved and concerned candidates. State Senator Judith Zaffirini told the *Laredo Morning Tim*es that she had heard anecdotally that mail-in ballots ran counter to early voting and Election Day results in the March 2018 primary election and that mail-in ballots were clustered by addresses, which raise suspension as if a person had gone door to door.

El Manaña reported that eighty percent of the mail-in ballots from the March 2018 primary favored two particular candidates, Patricia Barrera who was running for county judge and Melissa Joy Hinojosa Garcia who was running for County Court at Law II. County Judge Tano Tijerina filed an official complaint to the state Attorney General. Barrera was Tijerina's opponent and Zaffirini publicly endorsed Hinojosa Garcia's opponent, Victor Villarreal. Tijerina and Villarreal won their respective races. Tijerina said he made the complaint even though he won because voter fraud must be punished. Zaffirini said she despises corruption in all forms and encouraged individuals to report voter fraud if they see it occur.

In March of 2018, a local small business owner, Victor Gomez came forward claiming city officials retaliated on his rug business as an inspection was conducted. Gomez stated Councilman Alex Perez directed several local governmental agencies to raid his business as agencies from fire, health, environmental services, building services, and code enforcement inspected his business for what they called hazardous conditions. Gomez implied his business was inspected by multiple city departments as directed by the councilman because he did not support Perez in his bid for county commissioner and did not allow him to place signs on his business.

Instead, Gomez supported the incumbent, Wawi Tijerina and had her signs on his business. Perez's campaign headquarters was located in front of Gomez's business.

According to Gomez, former Councilman Juan Narvaez called him multiple times asking for the support of Perez, but Gomez declined. Gomez believed the inspection by city officials was done in retaliation.

In a council meeting, Ramon Chavez, the Executive Director of Public Services admitted Perez asked him to follow him to Gomez's business and asked Chavez to look into the business as he thought the items outside the place of business were hazardous and had received complaints from residents regarding the establishment. Council voted to forward the complaint to the Ethics Commission in which they ruled that Gomez needed to file a formal complaint before moving forward.

Once Gomez filed a formal complaint, the Ethics Commission dismissed the complaint, as there was not enough evidence that Perez was guilty of the retaliation charge. In the meeting, Perez's brother-in-law, Judge Joe Lopez spoke saying he was the one who contacted Perez complaint of the Gomez's business.

In July of 2019, the rise of social media in political opponents became publicly heated when County Commissioner Jesse Gonzalez sent his opponent, Louis H. Bruni a cease and desist defamation letter. Bruni posted on social media comments on what the letter states "accused" Gonzalez of "having an extramarital affair with Webb County Treasurer Raul Reyes and "committing extramarital homosexual acts with unnamed individuals." Bruni continued to make allegations on other elected officials on social media.

In the summer of 2019, The Laredo Ethics Committee voted to fine local activist and past city council candidate Vish Viswanath $8,400. Viswanath and small business owner Victor Gomez had filed a complaint against the city's two interim co-city managers. Viswanath's complaint was for an approval of water rate increases that alleged some of the monies allocated were not allowed by the city charter. Gomez alleged there was a conflict of interest between Councilman Dr. Marte Martinez and a company working with the city saying Dr. Martinez lied on his application for his city council candidacy about his indirect interest with the company. Martinez and Viswanath were in the run-off for the council race. The Ethics Commission dismissed the complaints voting that the complaints were deemed frivolous and fined Viswanath.

Citizens have at times been punished for speaking out. Evidently "*LaGordiloca*" whose real name is Priscilla Villarreal faced criminal charges in 2017 with two counts of misuse of official information, a third-degree felony for publishing information on a suicide and automobile accident on her Facebook page, which has over 130,000 followers.

Villarreal's charges were later dismissed in March of 2018 after District Court Judge Monica Zapata Notzon found Villarreal was denied due process because of the Texas statute used to charge her, which the judge deemed unconstitutional. Months after having her charges dismissed Villarreal teased running against Saenz for mayor, but later refused and endorsed Vela. In April of 2019, she filed a lawsuit against several city and county officials, including District Attorney Isidro Alaniz and the Laredo Police Chief alleging they violated her constitutional rights and claimed she was retaliated as she was wrongfully arrested.

On her page, Villarreal has accused Alaniz for protecting his friends especially in the *maquinitas* raids where she posted photos of Alaniz with several *maquinitas* owners.

Whether we like it or not, the government is not going anywhere and sometimes the government, be it local, state or federal will implement laws directly influencing your daily lives. The only way one can influence government on what they can or cannot do with their daily lives is to vote by controlling the issues and voting for those candidates with issues mostly pertaining to you. If there is no candidate, then you must take action by running yourself. Only you can influence your government, do not be afraid to stand up, organize, vote, and run - this is your democracy.

Charter initiative

On April of 2016, a group named Moving Laredo Forward delivered 10,513 signatures to city hall as the first-ever citizen-initiated charter referendum for the City of Laredo. The group made up of private citizens, and the Laredo Chamber of Commerce Legislative Committee proposed changes to the city charter to have hybrid at-large council districts and grant more power to the mayor.

The majority of the city council members opposed the group's idea and passed a resolution opposing the changes to the city charter. Councilmen George Altgelt and Charlie San Miguel voted against the resolution. Mayor Pete Saenz publicly supported the group and their efforts. Other public individuals supporting the group were Tax-Assessor Collector Patricia Barrera, IBC Bank president Dennis Nixon and Miguel Conchas, director for the Laredo Chamber of Commerce.

Moving Laredo Forward supported the at-large districts because they would give a voice to all citizens of the city and have representation from more city officials in the council rather than just one city council representative.

Those opposed stated this would take Laredo back to the *patrón* system Mayor Tatangelo fought and would give rise to more wealthy individuals serving on the council as running at-large campaigns tend to be more expensive to run. Local history suggests that in the 1922 and 1924 Laredo elections, all candidates running had no opponents and received the exact number of votes. This occurred because the city charter was amended earlier before these elections to have all districts, or wards at the time, run at-large, making it difficult for an independent candidate to be elected in these citywide campaigns. On the other hand, the population of the city was much less in 1922 than in 2016.

The group aggressively gathered signatures throughout the city, including Mall Del Norte, college campuses, and the Webb County tax assessor's office.

Ultimately, the group triumph in getting the sufficient amount of signatures for the referendum to be placed on the November ballot of 2016. Voters ultimately approved three of the five propositions. One of the two that did not pass was the most controversial proposition having to divide the city council into four single-member and four at-large districts with 55.30% of voters voting "against."

Chapter 13:

VOTES DO MATTER

Laredo and Webb County has seen many close races in almost every election. People say their votes do not matter; a sentiment not true based on the numbers. Many races in multiple fields of candidates often go into a run-off where the second-place winner is often a few hundred votes away from the third place winner, who could potentially win in a run-off election.

In 2008, Webb County saw one of the most interesting races in the Webb County sheriff's race with Martin Cuellar and Rick Flores. Initially, the Election Day count saw Flores losing the election by 37 votes. After a recount of the election, this saw Flores winning the election by 133 votes.

The Cuellar campaign said the numbers indicated something peculiar and Colin Strother, the campaign manager for Cuellar stated, "That big of a change is highly unusual, and there are considerable questions about the process."

This race was taken to court where State District Judge David Peeples ruled Martin Cuellar won the run-off election against Flores. Judge Peeples ruled Cuellar the winner of the runoff by 42 votes. Webb County elections used an electronic voting system for this election and were the cause for this controversy.

After incumbent Webb County Commissioner Frank Sciaraffa ran for reelection in 2012, he went into a runoff election facing Mike Montemayor. In the runoff election of the 5,812 votes cast in the race, Montemayor received 2,908 votes, or 50.03 percent against Sciaraffa's 2,904 votes, or 49.97 percent. Montemayor won the race by only four votes.

Sciaraffa asked for a recount, and ten days later, Mike Montemayor won the recount vote by ten votes.

In March of 2002, the race for the Webb County Democratic chairman was very close. A race between incumbent Robert Balli and challenger Rolando Herrera showed them neck and neck in the final result with Balli garnering 13,659 votes to Herrera's 13,689 - only a 30-vote difference. A run-off took place as there was an option for a write-in candidate and there were 107 write-in votes, which lead to none of the two candidates earning 50 percent of the vote in this close race.

There were write-in votes for Mickey Mouse, a fictional cartoon character that could have made the difference. In the run-off, Roberto Balli edged out Herrera to be re-elected as chair.

In the March 2014 primaries, justice of the peace precinct four candidates Yu-Hsien "Shen" Huang DelRio and Jose "Pepe" Salinas were only 89 votes apart. DelRio received 2,566 votes to Salinas' 2,655. The race had eight candidates, and these two went into a run-off where Salinas eventually won the race.

In the November 2012 City Council race for District 7, four candidates were running in this race. Jorge A. Vera received 44.50% of the vote, or 2,215 votes not enough to win outright. A run-off would be in place. However, the number two, Hector Lee Patino received 1,127 votes or 22.64% and the third-place candidate, Yolanda Salinas received 121 votes less to be in the run-off with 20.21% or 1,006 votes.

A March 2002 primary for Webb County Commissioner included three candidates, David R. Cortez, Consuelo "Chelo" Montalvo, and Miguel Urdiales. Cortez received 136 fewer votes than Urdiales and forced into a run-off where Cortez eventually won the seat.

The Webb County Constable, Precinct one race in 2004 between Rodolfo "Rudy" Rodriguez and Raul Hinojosa found Rodriguez winning with only 43 votes more than Hinojosa.

In the 2016 run-off, Webb County Commissioner percent one race, former city councilman Esteban Rangel lost to sheriff's captain Jesse Gonzalez by only 46 votes. This is the same race where it has been a close one other election years. Rangel filed for a recount where the result remained the same. Several weeks later, he filed a lawsuit against Gonzalez alleging fraudulent votes took place and some voters had registered addresses from vacant homes.

Chapter 14:

TRUMP'S LAREDO VISIT

Trump press conference with Laredo leaders.

Is it safe for me to get down (off the plane)? That's what Trump said as his plane landed at the Laredo International Airport according to Mayor Pete Saenz. Then, Trump saw a large crowd, some protesters, and some supporters to which Trump said "Hey, the Hispanics love me."

On July 23, 2015, Donald J. Trump, a Republican candidate for President of the United States of America visited the gateway city. He came in his private plane and greeted by several Laredo officials, including Mayor Saenz. Trump wore a white "Make America Great Again" cap all throughout his visit.

Trump's visit was broadcast live on CNN, Fox News, and MSNBC showing him talking in front of the mayor, city manager, several city councilmen, police chief and other officials. He praised City Manager Jesus Olivares by stating "I'm gonna steal him to run something for me..." and said they are tremendous people. He also did not know who "el chapo" is when asked by reporters, responding "the who... I don't know anything about him." He also slammed Hillary Clinton, the Democratic presidential candidate. The candidate's proposed border wall was also discussed and criticized by city officials.

One thing we learned from the Donald Trump visit is he actually wears caps, okay to get serious here, is he certainly knows how to create a media circus. Some people have complained about how the mayor and other elected officials could be with him and spend money for security and host the Donald.

Big name Democrats such as former Congressman Joaquin Castro from San Antonio even stated Trump just used Laredo officials to make him "look good."

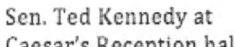
Sen. Ted Kennedy at Caesar's Reception hall

NBC reporter Chuck Todd came out on MSNBC stating, "This was sort of surreal event and what I found fascinating is say what you want about Trump, he showed some political nimbleness there figuring out how to corral the local officials sort of shrouding himself in the local officials and they played along and maybe they decided to make lemon out of lemonade and say hey let me say about how good Laredo is and we're doing great. You know not saying anything to agree with

Donald Trump but felt comfortable. I mean as far as an appearance you have to give Trump credit for making it look as if he's working with local officials, they were welcoming him with open arms- you gotta hand him that."

On the one hand, we can see this as the mayor and elected officials welcoming a major presidential candidate to our city. Why not invite potential presidents to visit our city? How did we know he was going to use us? Would it have seemed wrong to not even welcome him in front of all the national media attention?

Also, yes, money and resources were obviously spent during his brief but spectacle tour of our city. Money and resources of which are coming out of your pocket, right? Did Trump reimburse us for our money used? Is it even right to have him pay for our welcome? He is a guest; would we charge a guest coming into our home for a cup of water?

You see the right and wrong about this is not too clear. Going back to the 2008 presidential race when Hillary Clinton came down to Laredo campaigning for president in the Democratic primary against Barack Obama, she had a lot of city resources used for security and event, and many of our elected officials and former mayor were on hand to welcome her as well.

However, not one elected official at that time was there when the late Senator Ted Kennedy came to Laredo to campaign for then-candidate Obama. No city resources were used for his visit, and a private reception hall was host to Kennedy, granted it was not the candidate (Obama)

Hillary Clinton with Congressman Cuellar and Mayor Salinas in a 2008 downtown Laredo rally

himself but the late Senator (Kennedy) was a major power player at that time and eventually as we all know Obama, not Clinton would become president.

With this said, whatever your views or opinions on any candidate it is always a nice gesture to welcome someone to your "home" or in this case, city. If the guest appreciates your gesture or "uses" or abuses your gesture, it is a different story and one the hostess needs to address appropriately with all the mighty leadership they may have.

We should not stop welcoming or hosting candidates, as one day maybe they may just be president and Laredo may need them.

The question now is what is the limit in which we, the taxpayers pay to host and secure these candidates and events? At what cost? To what extent? What is the plan? Let this be a precedent to set a plan in place. Laredo is growing and we need to expect this as I am sure we will have more Hillary's and Trump's coming by in the future.

Throughout the campaign of Donald J. Trump, he had the support of IBC Bank CEO Dennis Nixon who fundraised heavily for Trump in Texas and contributed $2,700 to his campaign and $33,400 to the Republican National Committee.

Mayor Saenz also said he voted for Trump but opposed Trump's border wall plan and Trump's visit was important to explain how the wall was not needed at the border.

On November 8, 2016, Trump was elected as the 45th president of the United States. He captured only 22.5% of the Webb County vote. A week after Trump's election, Mayor Saenz and the city manager congratulated Trump and sent a note to him wanting a meeting to discuss trade and other border issues in Washington.

Chapter 15:

INTEREST IN LOCAL POLITICS

An interest in politics escalated during the 90's as a five-year-old when seeing my late grandfather, Jorge Casiano, Sr. involved in local politics. He was an activist and would speak out against the actions of elected and city officials on occasions. Having grown up watching my grandfather involved in politics advocating for the people and someone who was widely attentive to local politics and advocated for the common good.

I ran an unsuccessful campaign in 2014, not as a typical politician running for office, but to serve the people of Laredo and its future. I stated when running, "I am part of the future; therefore, I want to ensure that our future is strong and free of corruption, favoritism, and political pressure."

Change is often said in campaigns, elected official's come and go and those, the few who leave a legacy are the ones who seek change for today and tomorrow. Former Laredo Mayor Aldo Tatangelo left a legacy imprinted on Laredo even after he is gone. Those are the true game changers.

My grandfather fought against corruption after the tenure of Tatangelo was gone by attending city council meetings at city hall and writing letters to the editors in the *Laredo Morning Times*. He often spoke against the on-goings in city government in the early 90's in the Saul Ramirez administration and sparred at times with others regarding city issues. I remember seeing him involved in the community in this manner at a young age, thus became interested in what and who our elected officials would do or were.

Growing up before even stepping foot at an elementary school, I saw the pavement of a still unpaved street in front of my grandparents' home in Kearney Street, a dirt road in a centralized city reminiscent of the 19th century. My grandfather fought for this street to be paved and finally was towards the end of Tatangelo's tenure as mayor.

Vague memories are that my grandfather was never a hardcore Democrat or Republican but can remember he did support some Republicans in local elections. I do not believe it was much because of a political party, but more of a referendum on the norm or the usual old-time politics that he saw was still running in the city, as most elected officials ran as a Democrat.

While my memories were vague, I remember him supporting candidate Fernando Cantu, a Republican running for Texas Senate in District 21 against Judith Zaffirini, a Democrat in the 1994 election. I remember even helping place campaign flyers of Cantu in envelopes for a mass mail out. Of course, Cantu only received 31% of the vote, and Zaffirini eventually won re-election in this Democratic stronghold of Laredo and remains the incumbent.

I never fully understood his reason for not supporting Zaffirini but knowing he fought against corruption there must have been something he knew. In most recent times, Zaffirini has been found to influence University of Texas officials with her clout in

Austin on behalf of well-connected applicants. She is influential in higher education funding, and some believe her clout could have been used to secure funding for the university. Email exchanges between Zaffirini and Chancellor Francisco Cigarroa were released in 2014 and reported by watchdog.com.

Another report in 2013 alleged Zaffirini and other co-defendants in a lawsuit of gross mismanagement of a multi-million-dollar estate. The lawsuit alleged she forged documents and involved tax fraud and other schemes. Zaffirini's husband called the lawsuit groundless.

It would be shameful to just pinpoint Zaffirini as corrupt because in Austin, well corruption runs rapidly on all sides. Texas legislators only are paid $7,200 and have to feed off from campaign funds to pay for lavish perks and personal expenses, from well, special interests. Former Senator Dan Patrick, a Republican used his account to pay for $134 in clothing at Men's Warehouse for a photo shoot, while Zaffirini spent $2,000 of funds on Amazon.com for books. Go figure.

My grandfather never ran for political office as was disabled but always involved and concerned about our community. He was not one to commit political grandstanding to receive spotlight in the media or for political gain. To this day, people do not remember his name, but his actions and words ensured the political atmosphere of Laredo at the time to be aware people were watching them.

When asked by Laredo Community College President Juan Maldonado after my campaign defeat whom my grandfather was, he stated he did not know him. Of course, he was not one wanting his name on a plaque or a park named after him; he just wanted change for his grandkids, change that is still not seen.

My grandfather passed away in the summer of 1995 from a heart attack and could not see what the politics in Laredo would still yet bring. His cause of death at a young age of 52 sparks me to think if his physical demise had anything to do with his passion for his community.

As quoted from one of his letters, "Just as there is an answer to a question - there is a reason to an abrupt action...here today - gone tomorrow, and only the creation of our memories, good or bad, will be remembered by our friends and enemies."

Chapter 16:

MY CAMPAIGN IN 2014

I decided to run for public office in November of 2013 and place my name in the race for the Laredo Community College Board of Trustees in 2014. This was not an easy decision to run for office, as I knew I faced a lack of funds, name recognition, and my non-political personality. Never been one to crave the limelight or commit grandstanding, this is already a minus for being an effective candidate. Politicians are often bloodsucking, brown-nosing opportunists looking for any vote they can get, and then when elected they snub the people unless they are running for reelection or something else. I am not a fabricated politician looking for one's interest or personal gain per say; one will either support me for standing my ground or not. My interest in politics and the problems the Laredo Community College faced raced me to the answer – to run.

I finalized the decision to run upon seeing how Laredo Community College had at the time been at an unfortunate juncture of its lifetime as it faced declining enrollment, issues with accreditation, and financial problems.

I officially announced on Facebook "The taxpayers, the students, and the staff of LCC deserve better. I am not running to be against any opponent, incumbent or running for personal gain; this race is for you. You deserve an institution that is accountable, accessible, and affordable."

My campaign signs placed on a yard

My intentions were clear by the time the March primaries of 2014 arose, and the LCC board elections were nine months away in November of 2014, I had no idea who else would run, except for the already incumbents in place. I ultimately chose to run in place 8, where the incumbent Jesse Porras was running for reelection. There was nothing against him but decided to run in this place because he was unopposed last election and thought the voters needed a choice. From then I arranged my campaign to focus on the issues and what I would bring to the table.

Being the political novice at the time, I went to the ballot drawing in August of 2014 and noticed two other candidates running in this position as well, which included Jackie L. Ramos. Ramos had run unsuccessfully for Webb County District Clerk and we both communicated when she was running earlier that year in the March primaries. I had no idea she was going to run for the board after she had lost the district clerk race and came to me as a shock. Her candidacy in the same race was not expected and disappointed, but this is a democracy and the more candidates, the more people would have a choice at the polls.

From then on, I decided to make the campaign of mine stick to the issues and my plans for the college if elected. I knew it was a challenge being one of four candidates in this race that included the incumbent and someone who had already run for office several times. I remained strong and ran a grassroots or cyber-roots campaign targeting voters directly and remaining active in informing the voters of the many pressing issues on hand.

Dr. Juan Maldonado, the LCC college president, campaigned in support of Ramos, which I felt was not right on his part and felt a candidate being supported by him would only feed to the norm at the college.

I wrote publicly to the *Laredo Morning Times* on how there were "groups" wanting to control the board. You had the "Maldonado" supporters and the "anti-Maldonado" supporters; I ran as someone who would be independent. My campaign was a very low budget; only spending less than what is required to report by law with no expensive ads in newspapers or huge campaign signs. Every dollar of the campaign came from my own pocket and made sure it was spent highly efficiently and smart. I was able to buy 200 small campaign signs ordered on the Internet, four mid-sized campaign signs, four t-shirts, and some pens and paper flyers. That is it, nothing fancy, and nothing extravagant. No headquarters, no "*pachangas*," no expensive "*cañoneros*," no campaign workers. The only one running my campaign was me, myself and I except my father who helped stand in sidewalks asking people for their support of his son and placed signs all over Laredo.

I have always said how a candidate managed their political campaign for office financially is an indication of how they will manage taxpayer's dollars if elected to office.

During the campaign, I only took three days from my job to work on my election and would often campaign during my hour lunchtime from work. This was something not easy but had to be done.

Being the type of campaign it was, I managed to meet people and able to gather their vote because of me, not because of any favors or anything else. I told them all I would give them was my honest self on the board and work to the best of my ability. Only my honesty, integrity, respect and commitment would be promised I mentioned. If they wanted that, then they could support and vote for me, that is all I ask in return. I would stand in corners all over the city often time alone with my campaign sign in an attempt to be seen by the voters.

My slogan was "New vision. New direction. Next generation…" and in a *Laredo Morning Times* questionnaire, stating, "I am running because I am part of the future and concerned about the direction we are heading in. I want to ensure our future is not like what we have today; I want it better. We cannot allow continuing the status quo or going backward. True leadership leads and not follows thinking independently for the benefit of all. My only vested interests are the taxpayers, students, and staff of LCC. We need the judgment over political experience and practical solutions for the common good as the future starts now."

On Election Day, November 2, 2014, I managed to capture 13.45% of the vote or 2,888 votes forcing a run-off between Porras, the incumbent and Ramos, who was just a few votes short of winning outright. Election Day numbers saw me gather more votes percentage wise than during early voting. The campaign also managed to capture many votes from young voters, and the results surprised many. In some precincts throughout the city in parts of South Laredo and Mines Road saw me receiving more votes than the other two candidates in the race, placing second. After the election, many told me that they did not expect me to do too well in the election results, one telling me thinking I would only capture a few hundred votes. Instead, it was almost 3,000. A person also told me "well, I was wrong; you are not a fringe candidate."

I was proud of my campaign and glad I took on the issues many could not. In a candidate forum, I spoke against the high pay raises of Maldonado and the state the college was in with him being in the audience. I may have been the youngest candidate running but did not back down from speaking what had to be said, even if it was politically dangerous.

Moving on

After the election, I knew our college was headed to either the same direction or a new one depending on who would be elected. The near future would tell me I was right.

In the run-off, in elections place seven and eight saw Hilario Cavazos, the incumbent facing Michelle De La Pena; and Jesse Porras, the incumbent facing Jackie Ramos, respectively. In this run-off race, Porras and Cavazos supported each other and Ramos, and De La Pena campaigned together. As a sign of unity, I attended the swearing in ceremony of newly elected trustee Jackie Ramos and my former teacher, Michelle De La Pena.

Being in the audience that evening, I overheard a gentleman telling Mercurio Martinez, Jr, a trustee, "you did it" with Martinez nodding his head "yes." Of course, I knew what had transpired. Being part of the Old Party and wanting control of the board for certain agendas, he claimed victory, as the incumbents; Cavazos and Porras were not on his side. I was not too worried about the seat in place seven, knowing it was in place with an individual with good intentions. Politics is politics, it happens, and here at least my former teacher exercised to do what was right as witnessed in future board meetings. I was not going to be let down.

After not being elected, I still became active in the on goings at the LCC board of trustees. I attended a board of trustees meeting on January 22, 2015, where dozens of people attended and asked the college president to resign. Trustee Rene De La Viña requested public forum to be put on the agenda but denied by Maldonado. Many members of the community and college attended the meeting in the audience and outside the building as the evaluation of the college president was set to be discussed in executive session. The meeting was interrupted by protesters, including college professors, students, and residents. Most of the protesters were young individuals expressing their discontent with the college administration, tuition increases, and accreditation issues.

Although the meeting was in executive session, the board took action (voted) to appoint officers and members to committees without public input. They appointed

Mercurio Martinez as board president. The board meeting was in executive session after the meeting was originally intended to be open for a public forum, thus creating a larger array of protesters.

A protester was holding a sign outside the boardroom stating, "He gets a pay raise, and we get tuition spikes." A college professor at the meeting took a piece of duct tape and placed it over her mouth as a sign of protest against the lack of freedom of speech. College police officers outside the building were shunning away protestors yelling and holding signs, with some members of the community telling the officers, "excuse me, you are violating his right to protest." A college professor told one of the protesters "he's here waiting for a policy, his behavior is not appropriate and he is not even a student here…and?" None of the protesters were seen inside the actual board meeting and were outside the meeting room and building.

On February 26, 2015, I attended another LCC board meeting where several people spoke out against the leader at this college and were shut down several times by the board president, Mercurio Martinez, and the college president.

There was a high police presence at this meeting after a previous meeting saw several people interrupt the meeting protesting the corrupt practices at this institution. However, this meeting was different and had Attorney George Altgelt speak out on a grievance process. Altgelt mentioned in his public comment, "good news is Dr. Maldonado is great business, bad news is he's really bad for morale." Martinez interrupted Altgelt and referred to the college attorney where he attributes to the public comments to not refer individuals by their name or title. Maldonado then stated, "I object to the defamatory character and comments that Mr. Altgelt is making against me."

Newspaper clippings of articles relating the on-goings at LCC

Richard Geissler also spoke out regarding a newspaper article titled "new board, new vision" (reminiscent of my campaign slogan, by the way, and not what I intended to be) and how the board and administration were trying to stifle public comments to avoid listening to the public. He also mentioned they had just expelled an honor student for handing out leaflets on campus and about the turmoil at the college.

An LCC English teacher, who was referred to as a taxpayer and a voter at the meeting referred to an agenda item regarding current practices communicating directly with the board of trustees, which would limit communication between faculty and the board. He asked for more and open communication.

Former LCC Trustee Hilario Cavazos also spoke out against some concerns on staff interrogating faculty members and certain board members wanting to do away with the faculty senate. He mentioned there is a lack of leadership, various concerns, cover-ups, and disciplinary matters. He had paper work on a "cover up" that occurred for seventeen months involving two individuals. Cavazos mentioned the title "assistant vice president of student services," Martinez interrupted him saying he could not mention titles. Martinez stated, "If you are going to continue, I might have to actually have you step back and go…" Cavazos told him "what happened to freedom of speech in the constitution" and referred to civil rights and 1968, Martinez interrupted him again stating "if you're to continue on the same, I'm gonna have to ask you to please take your seat sir." Trustee Rene De La Viña then told Martinez "Mr. Chair, he is not out of order, he's talking about the history, he's not mentioning names…" Cavazos then stated, "I'll make it simple, and to the point, I'm asking for the resignation of the president of the college, Juan Maldonado for infective leadership." Dr. Maldonado stated, "I object to those comments as defamatory in nature." Martinez agreed saying, "so acknowledge".

My blood boiled on how can public institutions such as this one, people do not have the right to speak their minds according to the first amendment of the United States of America. There is nothing defamatory for having an opinion of someone in leadership on their performance and speak out in a public forum.

Issues at the college continued, the termination of the college president was put off and on. On September of 2015, five out of the four trustees voted in favor of his evaluation. Newly elected Trustee Michelle De La Pena, my English teacher in middle school, stated to the media she wanted to propose to terminate the college president, but it was not allowed. She mentioned a lack of communication was the main reason, and the termination of their chief financial officer was not workable.

Maldonado suspended the chief financial officer for claiming she used her position to intimate staff to get a "confidential" document about the college. Some trustees argued she did have access to these documents as her position allowed.

Trustee Jackie Ramos, who Maldonado publicly supported and campaigned for stated differently. She told the media she was glad about Maldonado's leadership skills and wanted to extend his contract.

The college faced unprecedented grievances and lawsuits during this time, and some trustees stated they would like to be focusing on the students. De La Pena stated this college was not a soap opera and should be about the students.

On February of 2015, LCC and through its attorneys sent a former college employee and now concerned citizen a cease and desist letter to not post anything regarding the college on Facebook.

According to the letter, the individual posted about the possibility of a shooting due to the frustration and anger of many people regarding the college. Their attorneys informed the individual to refrain from posting anything

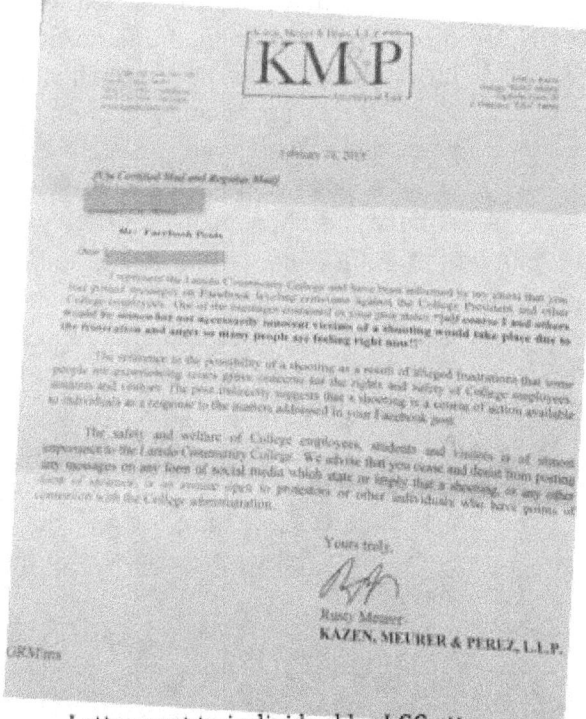

Letter sent to individual by LCC attorney

relating to a shooting or form of violence in connection with the college administration. The individual stated it was a shock because the posting only implied a shooting can occur with everything on going to college and worried about the situation at the college with recent protests, further stating the post was only viewable to friends and did not know how LCC administration and their attorneys got access to it.

The college also banned former board of trustee Hilario Cavazos in April of 2015 at the request of Juan Maldonado. Cavazos was banned from being on campus property for 14 days from April 16 through April 30, 2015. Cavazos also received a letter from their attorney; Rusty Meurer, stating the determination was made because of a recent pattern of disruptive behavior.

According to the letter, this was because Cavazos engaged in disruptive behavior needing his removal from the board meeting on January 22, 2015, for speaking to an executive session board meeting, closed to public comment. Cavazos told the media his constitutional rights were being violated and mistreated for speaking the truth.

On June 15, 2016, the LCC board voted 7-1 to buyout Maldonado's contract to retire earlier than August as originally intended. The board chose Dr. Ricardo Solis the previous month to replace Maldonado with trustee Cynthia Mares being the lone vote against.

This was not without controversy as the president's name was leaked to the media. On May 9th of 2016, the board selected a finalist for president of the college. The board president, Mercurio Martinez told the *Laredo Morning Times* that no consensus was reached on appointing a new LCC president on the 9th but the 10th, the following day, he told KGNS a "consensus was reached" by the board. The names of the finalist leaked to the media placing what Martinez called a "predicament." LCC attorney Rusty Meurer told the media no action was taken. Martinez stated the board could not make an official announcement of their candidate until after an interim period of 21 days per state law, however, later discovered that there is no state law prohibiting such naming.

Many at the college reported a breath of fresh air in the early stages of the new president's tenure compared to the previous president. In board meeting, he was seen communicating and listening to the needs of several staff members. He also made it a point to meet personally with every employee.

In January of 2018, Jackie L. Ramos serving as an LCC trustee decided to run for Webb County District Clerk against the incumbent Esther Degollado. Degollado filed a lawsuit against Ramos alleging she submitted signatures for her candidacy of district clerk that was invalid claiming discrepancies such as no valid names, missing voter identification numbers, missing signatures, missing date of birth information and some forgery of signatures were submitted. Ramos opted to submit signatures in place of paying the filing fee for a place on the primary ballot. The lawsuit settled with both parties agreeing to have Ramos' name off the ballot.

Maldonado passed away in January of 2019 in Laredo where a private ceremony was held.

Chapter 17:

MY LETTER TO THE EDITORS

Starting in 2014, I began to write several letters to the editor in the *Laredo Morning Times*. I always felt writing and expressing my opinion would jeopardize my employment or reputation because of how the political climate of Laredo is but decided it had to be done no matter the costs, this is the United States of America after all. Writing and expressing your opinion is a start to be a concerned citizen and participating in democracy.

My first letter published on January 16, 2014, detailed about the low voter turnout in Laredo and Webb County and coordinated with the on-going corruption we have witnessed throughout.

YOUR OPINION

Writer calling on apathetic voters, political activist to unite and vote for real change

To the editor:

Laredo has often seen low voting numbers in past elections.

Unfortunately, we have more registered voters than actual voters that go to the polls.

People have their reasons, positive or negative on why they do or do not vote.

From my experience, many reasons people respond when asked why they do not vote are how elected officials are typical and never get anything done; they do only during election season.

I believe that other reasons include favoritism and corruption, which many refer to in Laredo as the "patron" system.

Many of these reasons are heard through the grapevine from people who know elected officials themselves and how they do favors for one another, how one got a job because of a certain elected official, or how one got "away with it" because they know so and so.

I believe that this is the "you scratch my back, I'll scratch yours" deal.

These are several reasons why people do not vote.

I believe that often the same people vote in each election cycle, thus electing the same politicians.

Our politicians keep getting recycled in a way because of the group of people who do exercise their right to vote.

In my opinion, many politicians offer "change"; however, all that will truly change is the person in the seat.

I believe that the reason to vote is simple: your vote does count. The only way to change this so called "patron" system is to dismantle the usual politics as we know it with your vote.

I believe that we do have some elected officials and candidates who want to get elected for the common good and work for the people. It all starts with one to make those politicians accountable for their actions and not be afraid to challenge them.

I am calling on those apathetic voters and political activist to unite and vote for real change.

The minority (those who don't vote) are the majority so go at it — vote.

Sincerely,
Justin Allen Hundsnurscher

Another letter submitted to the *Laredo Morning Times* published on June 22, 2014, detailed how Laredo ISD board member, Jesus Martinez stated how a raise for paraprofessionals would be "money down the drain" and how paraprofessionals do not have "many responsibilities." I felt offended as a fellow paraprofessional myself at the time and had to defend us from this.

YOUR OPINION

Writer: Paraprofessionals are just as essential as any other employee

To the editor:

This is in reference to an article published on June 14 regarding LISD pay raises for paraprofessionals. I am writing not as a candidate for office but as a paraprofessional.

I feel offended by the LISD board member mentioning how the raise would be "money down the drain" and how paraprofessionals don't have "many responsibilities." This is a slap in the face and shameful. I sincerely hope this is not the sentiment of other people in power or leadership.

I do not work for LISD, but as a paraprofessional this cannot be more disappointing. We are just as essential as any other employee in a district and have numerous responsibilities that vary by department.

Every employee in a school district is needed for their position from the hard working cafeteria staff to administration. In fact, many paraprofessionals have a degree and still make a fraction to those of their counterparts. We are not here to become rich; we are here, committed for our students and just make enough to get by each day.

I commend Trustee Valdez, Dr. Nelson and the rest of the board for approving the much needed raise and keeping the budget balanced.

Sincerely,
Justin Allen Hundsnurscher

A September 12, 2014, letter to the editor published on how Laredo Community College employees spoke out in a board meeting asking for a much-needed raise. This is a grand example of how the community pressure on elected officials will get what they demand especially in election season. I felt some on the board were at fault for increasing the president's pay just a year before but nothing for their staff.

Writer applauds LCC employees for speaking up and coming forth

To the editor:

This is in regard to the LMT article from Sept. 4, "LCC employees demand pay raises."

Laredo Community College employees deserve better from the board.

There should be no need for them to go to the board and ask them for a raise, this should have been done long ago.

In November 2013, the board approved a $20,000 raise for the LCC president but not a raise to their employees, the classified staff.

Yes, their budget is tight, and we had a trustee not so long ago say the college is "basically broke," but what is being done about it? Almost a year has passed and not much has happened since.

The office staff, instructors and other employees of this great institution is the backbone of this college and are what make up LCC as they are dedicated to what they do; therefore, they must be paid adequately.

I applaud the employees of LCC for speaking up and coming forth, expecting the current board to take swift action to address this among of many issues on hand. Taking action should not require an outcry from the people or an election season. Leadership requires taking action for the betterment of all and being proactive.

This is why it is crucial to safeguard fiscal responsibility by examining the budget and expenditure patterns to prevent these occurrences. Increasing tuition fees and taxes is not the answer. Our students, staff and taxpayers deserve better.

Sincerely,
Justin Hundsnurcher

After not being able to capture enough votes to win an election for the LCC board of trustees, I decided to publicly thank my supporters by writing a letter to the editor on November 13, 2014. I felt entering this race was not a waste of time but rather a winning campaign because many issues that were brought to the table by my campaign were ongoing at the college and needed to be addressed. I looked into the future, and unfortunately, my campaign concerns on the college were true on seeing what occurred after the November election by some of the trustees in place and the administration. Someone told me after not winning the election, "don't you feel relieved you're not here" referring to being on the board with everything going on. No one will ever know how it would have turned out if I would have been elected and only one can assume, however, there are clearly many issues on hand and quite honestly the state of the college reminds me of the old *patrón* party rule under Martin, now it is just not City Hall, it is at the Elpha Lee West building.

Candidate for LCC board of trustees thanks campaign supporters and voters

To the editor:

I want to thank all voters who supported my campaign for LCC board of trustees having received 2,888 votes. The resources were limited on hand with a low-budget campaign, yet all my energy and heart were placed when running. Although this campaign did not receive the top votes, we were able to impact this race significantly. The impact from this campaign is already a win.

I did not enter this race to run against the incumbent or an opponent, I ran because I wanted to serve and be a voice on the board. Many issues and awareness of this race were brought to the table. I was fortunate to meet with many people, including fellow candidates. I wish all candidates in the run-off well and congratulate all whom won in these elections. Running for office is no easy task and requires dedication, commitment and honor.

This is surely not the end, but only the beginning. I will continue working to advocate for the betterment of not only the college but also our school district, city, and county. It is time we work together for all.

We also need to work on voter apa-thy. There are many registered voters who do not exercise their right to vote and many young adults who do not get involved in the elections process, and this is their future.

The elected officials we put in have a major impact on our daily lives, from the amount of taxed paid, local ordinances and laws we must follow and infrastructure of streets we drive daily. There should be no excuse to be apathetic in our elections. Be the influence and be involved, it's about you. Join me at facebook.com/ivotelaredo.

Sincerely,
Justin Allen Hundsnurscher

Asked by City Councilman Rudy Gonzalez, Jr. to serve in the City of Laredo's Historic District/Landmark Board in April of 2015 prompted me to become more familiar with many issues regarding our historic Laredo. In early fall of 2015, Laredo saw the destruction of an old historic building, the old Webb County Courthouse Annex and on October 2, 2015, I decided to express my thoughts on this in a letter to the editor.

YOUR OPINION

Writer: We must learn from this mistake and take action to secure our historic city

To the editor:

As the historic Webb County Courthouse Annex in downtown Laredo becomes a memory, we must now move on and learn from our history.

Unfortunately, the Laredo Historic District Landmark board could not have any say about the demolition as the structure, owned by the county, was deemed a public hazard, and the demolition permit was granted by the city without going to the board.

This is a very unfortunate situation that did not have to happen, if only county officials would have maintained this building throughout the years.

We must admit the county failed to maintain this historic building and let it die.

Officials came and went throughout many years and let this building crumble.

This structure got to a point where it was deemed a safety hazard to the public because nothing was done to preserve it.

Time was the enemy for this historic structure, but carelessness and in-competence were the ultimate death.

I hope this is a learning lesson for all officials that they must be proactive and maintain all structures to avoid a situation like this in the future, especially for historic structures.

A proactive, preventive, preservation plan needs to be set in place by all local governmental entities, Webb County, City of Laredo and the Laredo Community College, to ensure all structures over 30 years old are maintained and assessed periodically so this horrific event will not occur again.

We must learn from the mistakes and take action to secure our historic Laredo and Webb County for future generations to study and experience.

This is such a shame as our future generations will not be able to witness and touch part of our local history.

Current generations learn from history, and we must protect and preserve the past to learn from it.

Sincerely,
Justin Allen Hundsnurscher
Laredo Historic/District Landmark Board member

Chapter 18:

MY CAMPAIGN IN 2016

Early in 2016, I was unsure whether to run again for the LCC Board of Trustees in November of that year. Three positions were up for election, place one, two, and three. All had incumbents and individuals with high name recognition. Cynthia Mares, Mercurio Martinez, Jr., and Dr. Leo Cigarroa were all up for reelection.

On April of 2016, I finally decided to be a candidate once again and in place three against, the incumbent, Mercurio Martinez, Jr. I had discussed my intention to run against him to very few trusted individuals after learning what occurred in 2014 and remained silent on who I would run against until making it public on social media on July 20th.

Once the time frame for filing a candidacy was up in August of 2016, I noticed Dr. Cigarroa would not run and in his place two race had seven candidates, which I did not expect. Place one and place three had, Mares and Martinez, along with one opponent each, including myself in place three.

The decision to run again was tough, but the decision on who to run against was not. Many of the individuals I approached with my intentions to challenge were hesitant saying it would tough to take down a political *patrón*.

As President John F. Kennedy once said, we do these things, "not because they are easy, but because they are hard...". I knew it had to be done and was not going to let Goliath run unopposed. I told my supporters, "The stalling of new ideas and vision occur when we have the same person in office for decade after decade. The time has come to change the chapter and let others have the opportunity to serve."

Martinez has served as an LCC trustee since 2004 and previously served many decades in political office including at the former Laredo Junior College as a trustee. Those before me know and understand the history of the 1970's *patrón* system with the incumbent involved and why it was of such importance to move on from those who still plaque on from that dark era.

On an August 23[rd,] *Laredo Morning Times* article mentioned how I was born and raised in Laredo where my family struggled to make ends meet, understanding the economic situations of the taxpayers, where no silver platters were being served. I had never made it a point to publicly state my economic struggles growing up but felt it had to because many did not know me too well and only saw what they read, or try to read, my last name. My long and uncommon last name seems to put off some potential voters in this heavily Hispanic community, which I am part of and could not get away from family given name. Many voters admitted, they would just circle off on the ballot any Hispanic name in a race where they did not know too much about, especially in statewide races, for example, they would vote for someone named Hernandez and not Smith just because of the name. Thus, reminding me of how Representative Richard Raymond had to add his mother's maiden name "Peña" to his. This is just the way it is but entrusted the voters to make a wise decision based on the issues.

The issues were of grand focus on my campaign as I met with many individuals expressing their concerns about the community college they care and love so much. Each day I received calls from college employees, citizens, and even family members of professors and college staff who wanted to remain anonymous on the ongoing issues at the college. Many of the issues, such as employee morale, favoritism, low resources, and the budget all stemmed from the top with Martinez being the board president and occurring under his watch.

On September 24th, I attend a candidate forum hosted by the community organization Our Laredo. As expected, Martinez attended, and many pressing issues were addressed with the questions asked. Martinez told the audience at the beginning of the forum I had not done my homework, but little did he know what was to come.

One of the issues involved the lack of resources from the custodial staff as days earlier I met with several of the custodial staff regarding their concerns. Martinez never met with any of the custodial staff and attempted to sway this to other trustees who did meet with them and were on a special committee regarding the privatization of the custodial staff. There, I showed photos and information I obtained at the forum with Martinez being on the defensive. He denied these issues were occurring at the college even at other forums, such as the one on the faculty forum on October 19th where he told the audience the photos were not even from the college, which in fact are. One professor told me the photos he had seen were clearly from the college and could not believe Martinez had just said the opposite.

I could not keep up with the lies, contradictions, and runarounds of issues from Martinez; often time was thinking if this could be intentional? Could it be somehow that sadly his age was catching up to him? Or is this how a political *patrón* works? I went on to stick with the issues entrusting the audience, and the voters would see the truth.

On October 5th, I met with Dr. Ricardo Solis, the LCC president and two other supervisors of the maintenance department regarding the issues on hand with the custodial staff. He told me the issue of lack of resources was completely untrue and were "false statements" made by the employees just trying to get attention by being concerned and worried they would get outsourced to a private entity. Discussion about a private takeover for the custodial staff had been in the works earlier that year.

What was not obvious at the time of the meeting, is that days after I made the issue of the custodians public on a September candidate forum, the old equipment was being thrown out as directed by their supervisors.

There were two conflicting stories here, one with the custodians, the ones who are on the frontline and getting their hands dirty, and the other, which were the administration and the incumbent trustee.

As mentioned in a later candidate forum, I was not insinuating anything as I heard from both sides and just reporting it as is. The truth is there and obvious now.

The budget was also of issue. The college had a tight budget with the majority of the funding being generated through the dual enrollment program and non-traditional enrollment. The college's financial state was only surviving because of this and, therefore my platform included developing more vocational programs as many students were already graduating with an associate degree or going to a university and felt we needed to target students looking into going to a vocational career. The incumbent insisted the budget was excellent stating the college had a "double A rating," which according to him "was the highest rating" given possible, when in fact a double-A rating is not the highest; it is a triple-A rating.

Back pay was also owed to several faculty members, and the board had increased taxes for the past three fiscal years. I called for extensive budget workshops and cutting the fat. More funding from the state and lobbying for more money is also needed. The other issue was to look into expanding the taxing jurisdiction to include rural areas serviced by the college.

Meeting with several employees, many reported going through innuendos and feared retribution for speaking out.

I felt we needed to face reality and stop making up excuses. "The employees are not the ones making the college look bad in the media; it is because of some of the people who run the college in the first place." I was not going to run a campaign and say everything was fine and dandy because it was not.

"The house needs to get in order for our committed employees who just want to work in peace and want to be heard."

In what may have seemed like the normal political season, On September 30th, Martinez was honored at La Posada Hotel with the Area Health Education Center's lifetime community involvement award. Many present at the event were IBC executives and Mayor Saenz. On October 14th, Congressman Henry Cuellar presented a check to LCC of 6 million dollars as a grant from the United States Department of Education with Martinez being front and center of the media day event. Several weeks before the election, IBC Bank released a list of candidates they endorsed and encouraged their employees to vote for, including Mercurio Martinez for the trustee race. The *Laredo Morning Times* also endorsed him to no surprise. My campaign continued to go full speed ahead regardless of these political endorsements, political grandstanding, and political concealing.

My campaign on the other hand had a lone endorsement from the local Webb County Young Democrats. They represented many of our young voters and our future. Although the race for college trustee is non-partisan and so my campaign, I accepted this endorsement proudly as it is the young voters, regardless of their party are our future, and they should be front and center of decisions made that affect them.

An excerpt from a closing statement from a debate I attended:

> *"...The old Partido Viejo may be dead, but remnants of the mindset of the old patrón party still linger on today...*
>
> *We need more communication with the people, safeguard fiscal responsibility, keep tuition and fees low for students, not raise taxes by cutting the fat, ensure stability and meet the needs of instructors and staff, and be up to date with technology and safety. I'm not running to be a political puppet or master; I don't have any personal vendetta or special interest; I'm running and doing this because I believe in my heart to truly serve all of you.*
>
> *When a vote is up to raise taxes, I'll be there for the taxpayer because I know what it feels like to save every dollar possible and how we have families struggling to make ends meet.*
>
> *When a vote is up to help the instructors and staff, I will be there for them because I know what it is to live paycheck to paycheck, work under the conditions as a school employee, and needing the resources to do the job. I also know how it is not to be heard by those at the top... this our campaign not only mine.*
>
> *There comes a time to pass the seat to the next generation; it's time we move forward with a new vision and a new direction."*

On the election night hours before learning of any results from the race, I stopped by the city's Catholic cemetery and visited my grandfather and Aldo Tatangelo's gravesite just to have a moment and look back at what this race was for and guide me with strength. My nerves ran high, the anxiety of what was to come, and the mixed feeling of being relieved of the ending of a long campaign was all going through my head.

In a presidential election year, the voters turned out with my many polling sites experiencing long lines seen from a block away. On November 8th the voters had an ultimate say, I received 17,688 votes. However, Mercurio Martinez, Jr. was re-elected at the age of 79 for a six-year term with 61.89% of the vote.

I had no regrets running the campaign and no regrets speaking out for the countless people who could not for fear of repercussions. My only regret was not being elected, not for me, but because of them, the people I listened to and worked tirelessly in the campaign for. I was there for the people, did my part and then some. Being there campaigning in the rain trying to get every single vote possible. In the scorching sun, there unlike the incumbent who felt he did not need to and later we know he did not have to. A lot was sacrificed more than anyone imagines with the majority of my campaign expenses stemming from my pocket without receiving money from any special interests or political "*compadres.*" I received $425 compared to Martinez's $6,000 in contributions and outspent by him.

I worked tirelessly on being my campaign manager, advisor, sign placer, website builder, campaign designer – all me. All 10,000 mail-outs stamped on my own, all the website updated, managed, and created on my own. I did not have a right-hand man or paid workers; this campaign had a personal touch because it came from my heart.

The campaign had a good fight against a "*patrón*" and what many had told me was against a figure in the "Old Party." I made friends, I made enemies, but who cares?

I fought tooth and nail, literally as the ending weeks of the campaign an infected toenail irked with pain, but never refused to actively campaign. I was not alone as 17,688 other voters were with the campaign - something not many could achieve in a local race, being the third highest vote-getter in a 2016 local race, but unfortunately was still not enough to win.

After the campaign, the college began to see some change and realization. In the spring of 2017, the college president with the board's approval had a reorganization and let go of many top-heavy administrators; something Martinez had alluded to in a candidate debate, the college was "not top-heavy," which turned out it was. The outsourcing of custodial staff never came through, and one of the custodians received a much-needed promotion. Some of the less-needed services taking up too much money, such as an energy contract ended. Also, with the realization of the declining oil and gas business, the program facility was placed on hold and funds from this would be used for other essential facilities.

Slowly but surely the realization hit and some of the issues of the campaign were followed through making the campaign in 2016, not one in vain, but one that was needed, even if it meant not being elected and raising hell it did, I did, we did.

This is politics. This is a campaign. This is democracy. To everyone out there, do not be afraid, do not hold back, PARTICIPATE in your Government.

Chapter 19:

MY CAMPAIGN IN 2018

Third times a charm? No. Again? Yes. Run-off, of course.

LCC was no more as in May of 2018, trustees voted to change the name to Laredo College or LC. The primary elections of 2018 came and went as far as the general elections were concerned, November drew closer the municipal, school and college board races were arriving. As the start of the filing date approached to run for the November general elections, which included the Laredo College board races, I had no intention to run again. However, three positions would become open seats, as the incumbents would not run for reelection. Several people asked me to run and considered the issues needed to be addressed; therefore, the decision was made to run for the third time. I could not say no to the people and leave behind the issues that other candidates would not touch. I did not have "politicos" asking me to run, but rather faculty, staff, taxpayers of Laredo College, my run was not going to depend on politicians wanting a puppet, and my decision to run was going to be because of the people and how they got to know my platform through the years.

Some people would ask me why to run again for Laredo College trustee. Why not city council? Although I did not attend Laredo College, ironically, I feel that I had adopted the college from the years of advocating after first running for the board in 2014. My grandfather, Edwin Hundsnurscher was also stationed at Fort McIntosh during the war. Candidly, in my first campaign, I ran because I was interested in serving in an elected office; however, as a candidate for that office there was a responsibility to study the issues of the office and listen to the people who are impacted directly. I did. I did listen, I did study, I did prepare. As a candidate that is a responsibility and learned running to simply run and serve is not an option, but rather run and serve to make a difference is. Being the third time and several years of doing just that – Laredo College had been taken in by me as a valuable educational institution in our community in which I wanted to make a difference and have a larger impact for our students.

On an August morning, I went to Laredo College and submitted my official documents to place my name on the ballot for place 4. There had been no other candidates officially filed for this position yet. Only Annette Bonugli had signed up, but not submitted her application. Out of respect, I called her to tell her I was essentially running in the same position but said she would instead run against Esteban Rangel who had already filed his application for place 6.

Essentially, Bonugli said she had spoken to several "current elected officials" to help her campaign and defeat the incumbent of place 4, Allen Tijerina. At the time, I knew Tijerina was not going to run for re-election. Place 5 already had other candidates filed. I decided to place my name on the ballot as "Justin Allen H." and excluding placing my full last name on the ballot. Many would have trouble pronouncing and would already be called "Mr. H." by students and colleagues, others would confuse me as being a "*gringo*" and not being from Laredo, therefore not checking off my name on the ballot for this reason. After the run-off election, an opponent's official campaign volunteer would critique my use of the name on the ballot by posting on social networks how I excluded putting my full last name because I was ashamed of my family and heritage – something that could not be further from the truth. By the end of filing period, three other candidates had filled, Jorge "JD" Delgado, a local businessman, Feliciano Garcia, former mayor of Rio Bravo, and Roberta "Bobbie" J. Ceballos, a retired teacher. Delgado filed days after I had submitted the application; he had graduated high school with Bonugli.

This was the only race with four candidates, the most in all places up for election for the LC Board of Trustees. Once it was all done and the final minute of casting a name on the ballot was over, I knew there would be an uphill battle with three other candidates. However, I proceeded full speed ahead and grounded my campaign solely on the issues and my experience in education. I also touted my knowledge of the issues and the college after speaking to employees, students, and faculty throughout the years.

As the race proceeded, all of the campaigns were run clean, had productive conversations with my opponent, Ceballos who ironically is the mother to a boss of mine. We relayed how well and clean our campaigns ran, as well as how the issues in our platforms were similar and how we should work together if any one of us would win. Garcia did not actively campaign and participated in only one forum. Delgado was a candidate that seemed the next strongest based on the political connections he had and knew how having political allies translate to votes especially with the word on the street of how certain *cañoneros* were gathering support for him.

With four candidates, a run-off seemed likely, however my campaign felt strong because of the support received. The *Laredo Morning Times* endorsed my campaign, something that they had not done quoting "Justin Allen H. brings a youthful perspective that will help lead the college to higher performances in issues that count: enrollment, tuition, safety, and taxes…" *Laredo Morning Times* got it. They knew the impact on the issues raised in my campaign. Dozens of faculty also supported my campaign along with employees who were there with me in the last campaign. Many also told me they did not know the other candidates but had of me because of my past campaigns. Others stated Delgado did not have a sound platform and that I understood the issues. A faculty member told me, "You actually know what the hell is going on."

My campaign was active on social media and political signage where signs of mine were posted all over town in every part of the city. Many said my campaign had more signs than my opponents did. I understood signs do not vote, but it was good to get the name out further. Vandalism of signs were not seen much before the run-off, but after it was a different story. My signs were taken apart and thrown on the ground or vanished in several places. Others replaced by other candidate's sign. Of course, signs are simply signs, but they cost money and was uncalled for, but understood how it was full on post run-off political season in session.

During my campaign, some trustees supported my campaign. Nonetheless, I kept in contact with the rest of the majority of the board members at Laredo College, including two of my former opponents from other times I ran – Mercurio Martinez and Jackie Ramos. Unknowingly if these individuals supported me or someone else, but that did not matter to me. What mattered is that the connection was there and ensured that if I would win, there would an effort to work in unison to accomplish goals and my platform would be accomplished. Understanding how divided our local politics was, I felt I could bring them together and reach a common ground. The contact was essential to build a professional relationship.

As the general election came by, the results came in. I was disappointed in the results, naturally, but made the run-off in second place. I managed to get 31.54% of the vote, Delgado garnered 37.38%, Ceballos received 18.51%, and Garcia received 12.57%.

Immediately after learning of the results, I called Ceballos and endorsed my campaign. Garcia followed a week later endorsing my campaign as well. As the run-off advanced, the campaign was looking stronger based on the support and endorsements. I had support from all sides of the local political spectrums; local freelance social media reporter *"LaGordiloca"* also endorsed me. Ironically, not only did I have support from *Laredo Morning Times*, but also *"LaGordiloca"*.

My run-off campaign strategy was to capture the voters who supported the other candidates and target those who voters who did not know either one of us. I created videos and posted on social media, mailed out flyers to targeted voters, robocalls, and advertised on the *Laredo Morning Times*. My campaign outspent my opponent significantly in the run-off election and ultimately 70% of the campaign costs was out of my pocket, while the other portion were from small contributions and one from an in-kind contribution for signs from Javier Santos.

In the run-off, I also attended several social networking shows including one with former Judge Jesus "Chuy" Garza and a LGBTQ show OutLoud Laredo, in addition to two others with opposite sides of views from the current local political scene. I felt it was important to unify the community and that is what my campaign was about that regardless of the political clique you belonged to, I would be your public servant, listen to you, and govern based on what is beneficial to all of our community. A grand division of the local political scene was apparent where certain political groups were up against each other especially in a run-off. A hotly contested mayoral race and north side council race made the division in our local politics more apparent. My campaign was in the middle of all the commotion as it had support from all over.

However, a week before the run-off election, a photo floated around social networks and text messages showing my face in a caricature of a puppet along with other candidates and elected officials. A mayoral candidate, Roque Vela, Jr. was shown as the puppet master with other candidates and officeholders, including myself. One thing is certain – Vela never approached me stating he would be my ruler or manipulate my campaign, especially a campaign for Laredo College far off from city council chambers. The post became viral and heated with many defending me as the photo was uncalled for – people from all sides of the political spectrum. The photo showed how divided the political field was at the time with certain candidates running side by side. The campaign became more heated when my surname was being mocked by the opponent's supporters and belittled by my opponent's mother questioning my career while campaigning in public. Although winter season was coming, desperate season had arrived, and it surely felt like it.

Ultimately, on the run-off Election Day with all the nerves in the world and anxiety on how the results would turn out- the early results were released, and did not look favorable. The campaign was over. The longing to serve over. Everything was given to the campaign and exhausted many resources and energy in the fight. The campaign was long and strong, but the number of votes said otherwise. I was suppose to win this one. I would be lying to tell you losing is not disappointing. It sure is. It was time to move on. Oddly, hours within of knowing the results, I fell ill and stayed in bed for days just purely exhausted. The final results of the run-off election showed my campaign receiving 44.20% of the vote with Delgado receiving 55.80%. 2,398 votes set us apart. Precinct-by-precinct results showed me winning several precincts in district three on the heights area, southeastern part of the city, the Regency neighborhood, and Eastwoods area. This time around, I did not manage to get the support from the young voters as that went to Delgado. However, from analysis done, I received the support of the older voters, which I did not receive in my last election.

The day after the election, Mercurio Martinez called and left a voicemail congratulating me for a well-run campaign and wished me the best. Martinez also said he thought I would win. A lot can be said about his politics, but one thing is for sure - he saw through my longing to serve in politics.

Running a third campaign, one gets to know how the sausage is made to grab a seat in elected office. Our local politics has become a game of sorts, a contest to see how many groups of *cañoneros* a candidate can get and how many political allies can be forged. A candidate must determine which political groups to align with and which other candidates to associate. If you do not want to do this, then running for office is not for you. While public service may be the goal that is certainly not the result when running a campaign. Elected officials say, "it's different once you're in." The hot dog may look good, but you do not want to know how it is made. I was well intentioned, but politics got the best of this election.

In the succeeding months, Mercurio Martinez stayed as board president, Jackie Ramos was voted as vice-president of the board, and Dr. Henry Carranza was voted as board secretary. The LC trustees also voted to give up some of their responsibilities by granting more authority to the president by having the final word on hiring, firing, promoting, or demoting current or new employees. Cynthia Mares, a trustee spoke and voted against saying taxpayers and voters entrusted them to make these decisions and Trustee Tita Vela said by changing the policy, trustees are essentially not fulfilling their duties.

As of a year into the terms in office, there had been no agenda items sponsored by any newly elected trustee. They essentially have been there to simply vote "yay" or "nay" on administrative procedures and agenda items. However, photos ops are countless.

EPILOGUE

People need to understand the history of our politics; we need to learn from this history, old or current to make the future better and not repeat the same mistakes again. Just because one has a disagreement with someone does not mean you cannot work with them. A mindset of openness is needed in order to address the many pressing issues our community faces.

One cannot allow them to be associated with certain groups or have backdoor agendas because of their fear of not winning a political race or fear of retaliation. This is a country where we have young men and women devote themselves to join the military and serve our country because they want the rest to be free and allow us to speak freely.

Those, the few who do serve are the few and have the courage that many of us do not, and that is to serve our country. Running for and serving in elected office should not be about anything else other than serving your country too, the people.

Perhaps the culture that has developed has been so deeply embedded within making the average resident content in some fashion with the political norm of *patrón* style politics. The political culture that has developed could have made residents oblivious to what is considered corrupt and what is not. There have been cases where local governments have been corrupted for too long where citizens think this is just the way it is and is supposed to work because it is all they have been exposed to.

A March 2016 article written by John MacCormack titled "S. Texas a hotbed of corruption" from the *San Antonio Express-News* wrote on south Texas corruption. The article cites a one-party control of the political system, which includes political bosses, systemic election fraud, and voter cynicism. "Almost every government office seems to be involved in one way or another at various times," the article mentioned. Observations made from MacCormack pointed to combinations of "poverty, low salaries paid to public officials and police, the toxic effects of the drug trade and a cultural tendency to see public service as a means to personal wealth."

Our community has witnessed city employees under Mayor Martin to allow raw sewage to flow untreated into the precious Rio Grande River. Residents have been consuming unclean drinking water because of carelessness in Rio Bravo; freedom of speech has been sidelined in some instances at public forums; wasteful spending has been seen by our tax paying dollars, and a pay-to-play system has been obvious in front of our eyes.

Many elected and public officials have come and gone, but the old-time politics continues in one-way shape or form. Many past and current names of elected officials are not bad or evil, some have made mistakes, some have had bad judgment, and others simply want power. Corruption in an elected or public capacity is not a place to do this, if one runs for elected office because they want power because they want greed because they want to be corrupt – then they are in the wrong profession or position. Those who choose to be this, they will then become rotten eggs in this democracy of the United States of America.

You can be a part of saving our local democracy. Run for office, raise your issues, talk before elected officials at city hall or the county courthouse, write letters to the editors, join group discussions or community organizations, sign a petition, post on social media, report injustices, report fraud, capture corruption as it happens, do something.

There is grand apathy of involvement within the people. While we may never understand as to why this may be, some reasons can include that a significant majority of residents do not read the newspaper or follow their local news. Many work for local government agencies, which fear retaliation for speaking out or being involved, finally many are simply working too hard to make a living to be attentive to their politicians. We must not forget that those politicians are our servants and they work for us - the people.

Mayor JC Martin said it best, "A lot of people don't like to make their own political decisions."

We need to learn from history and ensure the mistakes committed do not repeat. Feared is how corruption in Webb County is a way of life and part of the culture, which is part of the community. It has always been this way as a form of tradition and could always be this way unless we change it.

History repeats itself; independent political groups striving to control and grab absolute power. The names of the corrupted changes, the groups merge and become more powerful while former ties dissipate, even in bloodlines.

Giving out the ending to a movie or a book is not a habit of me doing to an individual; however, the conclusion of Fernando Piñon's book *Patron Democracy* published in 1985 ends writing, "As Aldo (Mayor Tatangelo) nears the end of his second term… there is a good possibility that members of the old Spanish families, those with land and wealth, will reclaim city government. If this happens, it also cannot be determined what course city government will take." The book closes stating, "It might be different names, but the outcome could be the same."

One cannot deny that there is a long history of politics in Laredo and Webb County. The political influence surrounds our culture and runs in the bloodlines of its residents. Everyone is guilty because we are involved in benefiting at one point or another of political favor, an indirect action such as voting for a name and not comprehending the issues or background of a candidate. Everyone is a victim because we fall prey to the culture of politics in the community and affected by the misrepresentation and backdoor favors involved in political maneuvering.

We must do more than just merely talk about it or read about it, the corruption. We must take action and break the cycle, this does not have to be, and the old mentality of how everyone is related to everyone else needs to fly out. As a community, we must demand accountability and elect individuals with their hearts in the place of serving their Laredo, and for all – our community.

We cannot be victims; we cannot be accomplices to the corrupt practices of politics plaguing the community we all live in.

ABOUT THE AUTHOR

Justin Allen Hundsnurscher grew up with interest in politics and government. He graduated from United South High School in 2006 and later obtained his Associates of Arts degree in Criminal Justice and his Bachelor of Science in Business. Hundsnurscher comes from a diverse family background that includes German descendants. He ran for political office in the Laredo College board of trustees in 2014, 2016, and 2018 unsuccessfully. In 2015, he was appointed to the City of Laredo's Historic District/Landmark Board and has remained active in the community. Hundsnurscher is a career and technology teacher at United South High School, an alumnus of the school he now teaches in.

Bibliography

United Press International. "Laredo police chief admits taking bribes." *Laredo Morning Timez*, October 26, 2007: 1.

Aguilar, Julian. "Laredo Mayor's highlights city's image problem." *The Texas Tribune*, October 5, 2010: 1.

Balli, Phillip. "Former Commissioner Mike Montemayor sentenced to prison." *Laredo Morning Times*, January 26, 2015: 1.

Brezosky, Lynn. "Laredo residents silent of corruption." *Express-News Rio Grande Valley Bureau*, November 4, 2007: 1.

—. "Webb County Sheriff Democratic Runoff." *Free Republic*, April 6, 2008: 1.

everyday laredo. "YouTube." *YouTube.* 2014. http://www.youtube.com/channel/everydaylaredo (accessed December 5, 2015).

DiLeo, Michael. "Familia Fued." *Texas Monthly*, December 1, 1998: 1120.

You can beat city hall. Directed by CBS. Performed by Bill Moyers. 1978.

Segovia, Joseph Francisco. *Texas State Histroical Association.* June 12, 2010. http://tshonline.org/handbook/online/articles/pqb01 (accessed December 21, 2015).

Rodriguez, Mikaela. *Laredo Struggles to Put Corruption Past Behind It.* April 3, 2014. http://www.texasobserver.org (accessed December 10, 2015).

Time Staff Reports. "Ex-mayor Martin dies." *Laredo Morning Times*, November 12, 1998: 96.

Piñon, Fernando. Patron Democracy, Ediciones "Contraste", S.A.; First Edition edition (1985)

Photos obtained from Google Maps, Facebook, and YouTube, all other photos by the author, Justin Allen Hundsnurscher.

email- justinforlaredo@gmail.com